blessed

blessed

meditations
on a life of
small wonders

Ann Rennie

© Ann Rennie 2021, All rights reserved

First published in August 2021
by Laneway Press
Abbotsford Convent
St Heliers Street
Abbotsford VIC 3067
www.lanewaypress.com.au
info@lanewaypress.com.au
Instagram: @lanewaypress

The right of Ann Rennie to be identified as the author of this work
has been asserted by her in accordance with Copyright Amendment
(Moral Rights) Act 2000.

All rights reserved. The author retains moral and legal rights. Apart
from any use as permitted under Copyright Act 1968, no part of this
publication may be reproduced, scanned, stored in a retrieval system,
recorded or transmitted in any form of by any means, electronic,
mechanical, photocopying, recording or otherwise, without prior
permission of the publisher.

Cataloguing-in-Publication details are available from
the National Library of Australia
www.trove.nla.gov.au

Cover artwork by Fiona O'Neill
Typeset by Luke Harris, WorkingType Studio

ISBN: 978-0-6450070-1-5 (print)
ISBN: 978-0-6450070-2-2 (epub)

*For my father who liked the facts of words
and my mother who liked the fancy,
And to all those teachers who
helped me navigate the in-between.*

Preface

This book offers an ordinary happiness. It is a celebration of the blessings we share in our collective lives.

Blessed invites you into my life to share the joys and memories and ponderings of a woman who is, at last, wising up. There is an element of memoir to some of these pieces, where formative times and places indicate a loose chronology of events. Some pieces were written well over a decade ago and have been resurrected for their first public outing. Some are in response to the pandemic and its impact. Others have been previously published but have been updated and expanded so they speak to the now. A number of these reflect on my own family life, as a wife to Robert and a mother to Grace, but I hope they move beyond my little triumvirate to a more general application. I offer you something of myself in these pages – it is my way of making sense of the world.

The publication of this book validates my professional choice of employment as a teacher, whilst doing something beyond the confines of the classroom. Teachers occupy one of the most important professions because we pass on knowledge and skills to the next generation. We also pass on dreams and hopes, wonderings and what ifs because our job, after all, is fundamentally to open the minds of our young charges to the rich possibilities around them. I am a teacher of Religious Education and this colours many of the sentiments expressed here. *Blessed* is both worldly and otherworldly, recognising the transcendent as an animating force whilst mindful that we each find different ways to purpose and meaning. I am also an English teacher. Today, in class, if the students have to write a poem, I do too. If we want the next generation to be literate, we need to model what it is to be a reader and a writer. We can also model civility and good will and how to participate in the public conversation in a way that is respectful of various worldviews.

Under the global impact of the COVID-19 pandemic, there has been a reconsideration of the way we live and the priorities we espouse. We have been forced by isolation and lockdown to look inward and to dispense with some of those frills and fripperies we now recognise as not so important. Our sense of community has been reshaped. We are now attuned to a new reality, and in many ways, a simpler existence, more aware of the heartbeat of humanity.

I am a woman of my words. I believe in words that affirm and encourage, words that stand up and are counted, words that make us better people, that raise our sights to a promising future built on the cherishing of the here and now with each other. As you read *Blessed,* I hope this book of mine, in some small way, helps you find your own small wonders.

*Write it on your heart that every day
is the best day of the year.*

RALPH WALDO EMERSON

In a world that celebrates the next big thing, the newest look, the latest trend, the what's hot and what's not, this year I am going to look out for the small and slight, the soft and singular soul-shifting wonders that can change the colour and mood of a day. These are the little things that mean a lot, when our hearts soar with joy, when we witness the love of mother and child, when we are lost for words in a moment of awe. These are small wonders – where happiness and sometimes holiness is clothed in the habitual and humdrum; they are the affirmations that life is good and that we have much for which to be thankful.

A small wonder is the poem that exactly matches your mood. It is a twenty-two degree day in early autumn as the trees dress in garnet and gold and the world appears rich with invitation. It is the call from an old friend, the jacaranda waterfall in the back garden, a new version of an old song, the feeling of joy in simply being alive and capable and knowing that you are important to those who love you. It is the long blue day of summer and the strange swoop of serendipity that reignites dormant feelings and suggests other possibilities. It is the clever headline, the incisive cartoon or the quick wit of those who make us laugh. It is the scent on which old memories are resurrected and long ago loves peek into the present. It is the skip in one's step when anticipating the moment of meeting or doing. It is the reliable pleasure of a good long soak in the bath. It is the knowledge that you have agency and ability and a voice; small, maybe, in the din and dun of a noisy world, but a voice nevertheless. A voice trying to be heard with its own plain truth.

I will be looking about me and listening for the voices of prophesy and leadership and gentleness; voices that use words as wonders, not weapons. I will be mindful of competing narratives and look for the kernels of truth inside hype and hyperbole. I will honour words that stand up for good things and do not double deal or disclaim or masquerade as something they are not; hollow instead of heartfelt. These are of the weasel word variety recently identified by Australian writer Don Watson. They are the words of shiny superficiality, rhetorical ruse, obfuscation, words that trick and tempt and misgive. They are words that do not improve our minds or enlarge our spirits, mired as they are in a meanness that diminishes and humiliates. They are merely transactional, words without soul. Instead, I will enjoy the gentle balm of poetry and philosophical flights of wisdom. I will steep myself in rambunctious tales of imagination and derring-do and read books that make me want to write. I will use words that encourage, celebrate and affirm; words of endearment, of joy, of wonder, of plain old common sense and careful candour.

A small wonder is seeing the kindness of your child and knowing that, somehow, you have done a good job in making them that way. It is the song on the radio that brings the past prancing back in all its rainbow hues. It is looking at a beautiful painting and noticing small particularities: a signature colour, the brilliance of a fold of silk, the slight protuberance of a trembling lip, a tiny buckled shoe, lowering clouds. It is being clothed in a quiet confidence that things are going well and you are part of an enterprise that looks ahead. It is an acceptance that the here and now is to be grasped and shaped well. It is being happy with who you are and not having to jump through others' hoops for approval. It is the gentle grace of equanimity and an enthusiasm for funny little projects shared with others. It is being able to read and write and sit with a good book and ponder. It is the mystery and intrigue of the imagination which can open up thoughts that are frighteningly large and exquisitely small. It is being chuffed that your brain is still whirring and that you can solve the nine-letter word problem in the morning paper – most days!

This year in my harbouring of small wonders I will succumb to the gentle joys of cloud watching and the chortle of the kookaburra in the old gum tree. I will listen to the rhythm of the rain and marvel at the innocence of a toddler's gummy smile and the giggling that goes with it. I will listen to my daughter as she tries on her dreams for size and I will notice the child who does her best every time, although she does not win the glittering prize. I will encourage the shy and sweet and will not be fooled by the false triumphalism that bigger is better. I will stoop to smell a grandmotherly rose and stop to exchange a cheery word with my neighbour. I will notice the sounds of life around me – the big brass band of getting through the day, the orchestral swell and hum of evensong and the jazzy interlude of unexpectedness.

This year I will learn to accept the small wonder of a compliment. I will notice the colours around me, peacock blue and fuchsia and sun-spun yellow, and be glad for the never-ending palette of creation.

I will submit breathlessly to the star-spangled soup of country skies at night and the cool complicity of moonlight. I will be thankful for the kindness of the colleague who bakes banana muffins and brings them in to share. I will be glad of the cup of tea my husband makes me when I am running out of puff in the evening. I will continue with my own small wordy adventures, dallying delightedly in old tomes and new texts. I will be in awe of the men and women who are humble and resilient and do small wonders when they care for grandchildren, deliver Meals on Wheels and refuse to use age as a reason not to get involved in life swirling around them. I will watch as the next generation innovates and creates, and I will wonder aloud how they thought of such things in the vast realms beyond my own understanding.

Small wonders can be found in the shelter of the predictable pattern. They sparkle in the ebb and flow of the ordinary. Occasionally, they are scintillas of surprise that choreograph change. They are fragments, vignettes, moments of glad grace that build gratitude and delight and give life meaning. Small wonders are alive in the first snowdrop of spring, a child's finger painting, the courtesy of a gangly teenager holding the door open when your hands are full, the tickle and fizz of champagne on a sunny afternoon with good friends, exploring a new neighbourhood, the rainbow after rain. Small wonders are about noticing the decorative marginalia and not being unthinkingly importuned by the bold and the brash of the attention-seeking. They are rewards for noticing. Small wonders are often clothed in humility and reticence, their delight enjoyed by those who look and learn and listen and linger.

They are a different way of leaning in.

Small wonders are moments of recognition and revelation – moments when we are bathed in an inexplicable exhilaration, a sliver of joy, the diamond moment in the duller duties of the day; when we see 'a world in a grain of sand and a heaven in a wild flower', as William Blake wrote. It is when smallness is somehow magnified, amplified, universalised into an amazing all-ness.

The French writer Muriel Barbery asks: 'Where is beauty to be found? In great things that, like everything else, are doomed to die, or in small things that aspire to nothing, yet know how to set a jewel of infinity in a single moment?' (*The Elegance of the Hedgehog*, 2006). I am searching for such moments this year as I seek out the small and wondrous. So, I will try again to jump at opportunities and be more spontaneous and led by occasional whimsy. That load of washing can wait, but this bright blue day will not. I will notice the change of seasons, the ladybird on the leaf, the new songs being sung. I will try to be a good friend, holding onto the friendships that have held onto me. I will colour the year with gratitude for what I have, and I will be glad for others. I will lift up my heart. I will jump for joy. I will be excited by the world around me and what it offers. The road less travelled will beckon me with its serpentine trails and faint tracks and Do Not Enters and I'll visit China to walk along the Great Wall.

The Benedictine nun Joan Chittister suggests that one way of coming to live the good life is to do one thing a day for the soul, one thing a day for the heart and one thing a day for the mind – a perfect trinity of endeavour. I will remove 'someday' from my vocabulary and replace it with a definite date, place and time. I will offer time to causes I believe in. I will watch movies with my daughter and visit galleries with my husband and carve out time on the weekend to wrestle with words. I will laugh and conspire with my siblings to plan the years ahead. I will continue to read voraciously, thankful for all the good words that inspire me. I will wear my bright pink lipstick and remember the importance of playfulness as a salve against seriousness. I will pray, raggedly and hopefully, believing I am heard. I will start the year, as the psalmist writes, with a clean heart.

The writer Annie Dillard reminds us that 'how we spend our days is, of course, how we spend our lives' (*The Writing Life*, 1998). So, this year I will look about me. I will be alive to small wonders, the wonders that dress our sometimes wounded world in the shimmering threads and shook foil of the beautiful, the truthful and the good.

This is an edited version of an article previously published in *Melbourne Catholic*, February 2018.

... time's thievish progress to eternity ...

WILLIAM SHAKESPEARE, *Sonnet 77*

As a woman of a certain age, the speeding up of time is giving me renewed clarity about what matters to me. All the time in the world is no longer how I measure my days and so this year I plan to not be wasteful of the gift of time. This does not mean I have to be productive every waking minute, but it does mean that my time and how I choose to spend it is a special commodity. It is the currency that matters most to me now.

Most of my time is spent at work. So, this year I will make the best use of my time with those with whom I am employed. I will not whinge or moan too often because what I do is meaningful. I like to think that, in some small way, I am building the future ... that my students will be the poets and philosophers, doctors and decorators, activists and artists of the next generation; that I can bring out the best in those who may still be diffident and shy with a little timely encouragement and the patience that understands the slow burn that ultimately becomes success. I will rely on the data of actually knowing the students in front of me. I will aim to help them reach beyond their grasp in their acquisition of skills and knowledge and an appreciation of all the world has to offer.

Work may not define us, but it says much about who we are. I will endeavour to be collaborative and sharing and fun and realistic. Theologians speak of the sacredness of the workplace and that the work one does confers a special dignity. How we approach this work can inform everything else around us. So, this year, although it will be the *same old, same old*, I will reinvent my relationship with work and reinvest my time there. I will acknowledge that I am personally well matched with my job – I can be a bit theatrical and a tad loquacious whilst ensuring that I cover a mandated curriculum in my own fashion. I know that some of the things I say will take seed and flower later, perhaps so much later that I will never know that my words did indeed hit their mark. Time will do its magic work. I will dutifully attend meetings, although my mind will wander and I will doodle and jot thinking about pretty words and how I can get some poetry into and out of my budding writers in Year 7.

This year I will be grateful that I am gainfully employed, even when it's hard to get up on a Monday morning and I have five classes on, tram duty and a meeting after school. I will be glad that I have agency and ability and that I can laugh with others and that the decisions I make are not globally important. I will talk to my students about leadership, teamwork, citizenship and how we must get along with each other if we are to take the human story forward. I will try to get smart with technology even though I joke that the only device we really need is the one between our ears and that it is switched on and receptive to the world.

I will belatedly acknowledge that Zoom has enabled me to stay in contact with my students to maintain connection and cheerfulness as the ravages of the pandemic played havoc with the norms of classroom teaching in 2020. Yes, I delivered content and instruction, but more importantly, I aimed to be a constant and predictable presence in a world of uncertainty. As an adult, it was the least and best I could do for the children in my daily care ... even at a distance.

I will try to mix things up a bit, although I am teaching the same book at the same year level as I did last year. I will look to the big picture of what I am doing but will also notice the small improvements in what a student does and comment on them so that they will be encouraged. I will ask for help when I need it, overcoming years of reticence and a certain embedded obstinacy that doesn't want to rely on others – or go to doctors! I will realise that I am not immortal and invincible and that I do not have to be an Energizer Bunny all the time. I will revel again in good books and good conversations and be glad of my good husband who stands by with good grace.

The fast lane has become too challenging for me. I am not ready for the slow lane. I just want my own lane. Perhaps, as I negotiate the latter part of my life's journey and look for new scenery to add colour to the old, I am becoming a little less acquiescent. I am not getting grumpy, just wanting this later chapter to make interesting and unexpected detours. I am taking charge and looking about me with curiosity.

This year will offer me its marvels, its days of wonder and its days of woe. Mostly it will offer me its days of weekly work and the occasional night-time corrections of grammar and spelling and gentle suggestions for improvement in a student essay. I will also spend this most precious of currencies on doing the things that matter to me. So here you find me on a Monday morning under the dome at the State Library of Victoria, suitably masked and distanced from the few others who have booked in for a three-and-a-half-hour session.

I couldn't be happier. I am fiddle-faddling with words and ideas, sifting and sorting, enjoying a cerebral humming. I am reminded of Shakespeare's quote about time's thievish progress to eternity. Time is on the wing. So I am spending these joyously stolen moments at a large old desk lit by a green light with scribbled notes around me and my mind brimming and buzzing. Helen Garner's words are inscribed on the wall near me: 'To slide into the Domed Reading Room at ten each morning, specially in summer, off the street outside, was a sensation as delicious as dropping into the water off the concrete edge of the Fitzroy baths'. I, too, slid in at 10 am, but with a summer grizzly grey and contrary outside. However, I am enjoying the warm wraparound delight that comes with the delicious sensation that my time is completely and utterly my own – for now.

Australians all let us rejoice ...

PETER DODDS MCCORMICK, *Advance Australia Fair*

I am spending most of the summer holidays on the balcony. Under my shade umbrella and perched on an old wrought iron chair, I can survey all around me with contentment. It may just be a neighbour's backyard pool and clothes crisping on a line strung between two trees and the silver gleam of a train as it passes and the spire of a church in the distance and a general greenery, but it's my view to enjoy. I can sit here for hours, companioned by the neighbourhood sounds of a child talking or a bit of talkback radio or the chirruping of birds in an airy sort of musical interlude. All I need is a cup of tea, a book to read and a mind briefly untroubled by the timetable of my working life.

The breeze riffles the newspapers, birds chortle happily and dragonflies and butterflies loop-the-loop in a crazy choreography. The sky is the blue of forever and no clouds spoil the cerulean swatch that gently girdles the suburbs. White and blue agapanthus nod cheerily ready to endure the heat. I can hear the putter and purr of the Ventura bus at the corner of the street and the chug of the train as it clatters purposefully in its sixty second run between Mont Albert and Surrey Hills. I am in the middle of the suburbs in Melbourne ... and could be anywhere in the world.

My husband often tells me that holiday is a state of mind, so I transport myself to Sorrento, Italy or the Peninsula, and enjoy the good things. With a croissant I am in Nice; with a few olives I am in Barcelona. The book I am reading puts me into make-believe Kingsmarkham where Chief Inspector Wexford is solving crime in a place that no longer resembles that green and pleasant land, England. I travel in my mind and it's priceless.

My daughter is at the local pool. My husband is dozing to the cricket and I'm just doing my thing, unhindered. I've been out for a morning coffee and the papers – there are some rituals that can never be tampered with – and have some idea about what is happening in the world because I have the time to read the commentary and analysis, and not just skim through headlines as I do the rest of the year. It's scary as global tensions rise with fear and panic, borders and alliances shift and political power divides and undermines. I know that what I can do daily, in my small sphere of influence, will not change the world, but it will change my world and those that intersect with it.

For the next few weeks, the only timetable I run to is an internal one. Soon enough the pulsating beat of the urban jungle with its staccato urgencies and improvised importance will become the relentless rhythm of the year. But for now, I can pursue my small pleasures, replenished a little, fortified by the luxuriance of the occasional afternoon nap, the seeing of friends, the pleasure of reading and writing, a few days in Bendigo, watching old black-and-white British movies, going to bed after midnight and not getting up at 5.45 am to get to work early to check my emails, do some photocopying and plan the lessons for the five-period day.

Once the door is slammed on the sun-kissed somnolence of these long languid drowsy days, these days when time pools expansively, I'll be ready to jump to the tune of my masters. The hours will become short and tight, sixty minutes' worth of accountability and productivity with little room for daydreaming or the poetry in motion of the mind left to wander. Data will drive reports and all sorts of performance metrics and I'll tick the boxes that few will bother to note.

Holiday time is qualitatively different to the time we spend at work. It is the time we allow ourselves to be a little playful, less stressed, more in tune with who we really are. We do not have to look or be busy. We do not have to perform or reach a benchmark or attend a meeting where decisions have already been made.

We can simply be.

Australia Day will mark the end of this idyll. My umbrella is festooned with the Australian flag as I seek shade under its Southern Cross. My daughter tells me it's bogan, but for me it's just practical and not a nod to extreme patriotism of the ugly kind. At night, on these balmy evenings, I can pick out the constellation in the celestial slideshow above, with nought to disturb my reverie but small nocturnal settling sounds: bats swooping, flowers sighing, the invisible threading of a silver spider's web on the flywire, an orchestra of crickets providing a bedtime lullaby, the hum of a radio, the soothing sounds of life breathing in and out; the exhalations of the day done.

The world turns, with its threats and fears and war wounds and its beauty and grandeur and hope, and for these few weeks I count my blessings. I balance, accommodate and jigsaw-fit all the differently configured activities that colour this temporary freedom. I will surrender at the last possible moment.

On an overcrowded, sorely-in-need-of-a-spruce-up-sixty-year-old balcony in an anonymous block of flats in the suburban heartlands, I indulge in my summer dreaming. These imaginative excursions will keep me sane during the coming year as it rushes ever faster to its end. My sparkly summer dreams may recede as my working year progresses, but they are there tucked snugly into the back pocket of my heart, ever ready to come out to play.

This is an edited version of an article previously published in *The Secret Garden of Spirituality*.

Things which matter most must never be at the mercy of things which matter least.

JOHANN WOLFGANG VON GOETHE

As I enter the New Year, with the surprises and delights of its verily unscripted days, I am thinking of the various speeds in my life: the days that hurtle by in a blur; the holidays where I can step off the motor for a while; the speeds that differentiate between keeping all the balls in the air, frantically juggling, or logging off with a relieved sigh; the speed dictated by digital time-lords, and the speed of light that is millions of years old and twinkles knowingly in the infinite inkiness of the night sky.

Today, time keeps us all in its tight-fisted and tyrannical thrall. We clock on and off. We run to a timetable, squeezing more in, being caught up in self-appointed urgencies, proving our worth by the hours we put in, the busyness we create, the drama of being all things to all people. We have forgotten time's humble beginnings when it had little to do but turn the page of ancient history as the sun came up. It is now a warrior, annexing and conquering the vast uplands of the imagination, ravishing the last preserves of the poet, prophet and philosopher; those who need time to think and muse and set us right about who we are and where we are going.

Time rarely pools gently around us. Rather, it must be regulated and measured, drawn and quartered, ensuring that not a bit of it is wasted. We can no longer daydream. We are in robotic thrall to here and now and hurry and quick and deadline. How I long to take my time, to slow down, saunter and stoop, to notice the small things ... to have, as the saying goes, 'all the time in the world'.

The lighting of a candle at St Francis', the late evening reverie that moves us into a more thoughtful realm, the quick prayer of gratitude, a slow stroll in a park noticing the chartreuse lick of green on leaves, gazing at the confetti of the cosmos – these are the times that build us interiorly. This is where mystery and wonderment and solace abide; a sacred space where grace lives. These moments allow us to step into another dimension, to log ourselves off from the enslavements of timetables and time trials, to grasp the freedom of true time out.

My husband knows that if I am having quiet time, I am reading or writing or thinking, sometimes about things of a soul-stirring nature, sometimes about pragmatic things, sometimes about nothing much at all. Just the mental sifting and sorting and storing that are best done without too much distraction; the casual collecting of my thoughts in the butterfly net of borrowed time during the first three weeks of January. I hear comforting neighbourhood noises, Smooth on the radio, the hammering of a cubby being built, the whirr of the washing machine in the shared laundry, my daughter laughing over YouTube clips and cat memes, birds skittering from tree to tree. I watch the clouds curl across the sky in a downy dreamy cavalcade.

Back on Earth, things trend on Twitter in a permanent present, a 24/7 stranglehold where history is what happened half an hour ago. That lovely old saying – 'in the fullness of time' – with its hint of completion and fruition seems to have become an anachronism because time no longer unfolds as it should, with sufficiency and elegance, but is cruelly wrenched open by immediacy and instant gratification in a world that counts itself lucky for something to go viral.

Time is the most important currency we have so we must be mindful how we use it. We know that we need to slow down, be attentive, mindful, present, attuned

– a veritable kitbag of words for self-realisation – if we are to have any insight into how and who we are in the world. We acknowledge how hard this is in a world that demands visibility, availability and immediacy. Where is the time for musing and mulling, for the deep delights of time untrammelled, for good old-fashioned cogitation which is not the sole preserve of old codgers?

If we are to remake ourselves this year, we need to renegotiate our relationship with time. We need to spend time with those we love. We need to make time to listen to the voices that remind us that we are blessed in a world that is burdened. In our haste to always be doing, and to be seen to be doing, we run out of time for the things that really matter.

So, a small sliver of softly slowly on a busy day recalibrates my internal chronometer and I get back on the merry-go-round. Such timely moments are the grace notes in the busy plainchant of everyday life.

Live in the sunshine,

swim in the sea,

drink the wild air.

RALPH WALDO EMERSON

We Australians love the beach, that great gritty welcome mat that encircles this island continent. Many of us have beach memories that curl happily into the past – honeyed days of togs and towels and icy poles. Especially after Christmas, we desert our suburbs, and their stolid reminders of routine and responsibility, to adopt a more languid, slip-slop-slap state of mind. We prostrate ourselves on a sun-baked altar. Sometimes we walk along piers and jetties, promenading with loved ones, gazing out to sea, casting a line, watching boats glide and skittle, jumping off the deep end, seeing sea and sky merge seamlessly on the horizon, wishing on a star.

Opposite the terminus of Adelaide's Glenelg tram line, I spend a number of happy and informative hours in the Bay Discovery Centre, learning new things and relishing the old. Located in the old Town Hall, the centre tells the story of the founding of Adelaide, and the people and events which become part of legendary local lore. For example, the first ever Royal Tour of Australia was in 1867 and started here when Prince Alfred, Duke of Edinburgh, the second son of Victoria and Albert, disembarked for an incident-packed three-month tour of the colonies. Apart from doing his duty, Albert also managed to go incognito as he visited more colourful and less salubrious establishments, events not reported back to *The London Illustrated News* and its polite society readership.

But rather than big picture history, I am interested in the personal and the ephemeral, the small and telling story, the interesting cameo. People have sashayed and sauntered along the Glenelg jetty for more than 160 years; some hoping for a good time, others glad for time off work, others not expecting the surprise collision of two hearts. They have been, as we will be, part of the passing parade; that great ensemble work known more generally as *life* and eternally choreographed by that capricious mistress, Fate.

The original jetty, with its Pavilion Tea Rooms and Aquarium, was badly damaged by a storm in 1948. Today it is a far more modest construction and those who walk along its short stretch no longer have to dress up to be seen. In the Discovery Centre, a fascinating exhibit displays the underwater plunder recently excavated by divers from around the jetty. These recovered items provide an insight into the leisure activities of this petticoat past and, for me, provoke a certain curiosity as to how they have come to nestle in the sand at all.

Included in the seabed archive are thousands of teaspoons, mustard spoons and cake forks, along with crockery, earthen and glassware. There are keys and buttons and glasses and lipstick cases, dress pins, hatpins, badges and brooches, pendants, lockets and charms, pen knives, membership medallions and tokens for the short-lived Luna Park (1930–1934). There are cuff links and collar ties, suspenders and sinkers for fishing. There are neck chains and bracelets and badges, watch chains and photographic accessories and assorted ammunition. There are stoneware jars for ginger beer, cast iron toys, whistles, wheels, a tiny ceramic doll's leg, locks, stoppers, hinges, screws, nails, syringes, marbles and board game counters. It makes one think deeply about what people carried or hid in bags and wallets and pockets and picnic baskets on their afternoons out. Perhaps we have been fooled that the past was as idyllic and innocent as the postcards pretended. Perhaps we have been gulled by the fake news of a prettily revisionist history that purges the insalubrious from the dot points and dioramas of the not-so-long-ago.

What really gets me thinking, though, are the number of rings recovered from the watery grave below the jetty. That gold wedding ring now somewhat dulled because of its briny burial – was it accidentally dropped or hurled furiously? What of the ring engraved 'Lucy Birmingham 1881' or the one with the single initial 'C' or the number of dainty Victorian dress rings with garnets or tiny seed pearls missing? Every item has a small snatch of human story appended to it, but these have been lost to the tumult of unforgiving time and tide.

How intriguing this trawl through Glenelg Beach, a century ago when the pier was packed, ferries steamed past and objects were lost irretrievably through gaps in the wooden planks. So many stories have been lost to shifting sands. It reminds me of that long ago day at St Kilda Beach when my sister Rose and I were in our late teens and sunbathing carelessly as we all did in the late 1970s. Kicking over some sand as we lay out our Dickies towels, she found a sterling silver bracelet. There were no identifying marks; nothing to say how long it had been there or who was forlorn because they had lost something precious. Nothing to say who had thrown it away in a fit of pique. Nothing to say that it had slipped off a dainty wrist at the end of a lovely day. Nothing but a hallmark. So, it was *finders keepers* as the sand divulged its long-buried secret. After Rose had duly admired it, I asked for a closer inspection. I snatched it out of her hands and have worn it on and off for forty years since. It now sits in my daughter's jewellery box, waiting until she feels inclined to wear it. She knows of its unexpected finding, our little bit of treasure trove, picked up when we were young and foolish and ice cream dribbled down our chins and fish and chips wrapped in newspaper was a wicked treat as we trammed back home to the eventless leafy middle suburb of our childhood.

We Australians know the joys of the ocean and the welcome mat of beach; that democratic strip of dune and sand and ti-tree, of rock pools and shallows and the tickle of seaweed; that great lapping and swelling font where all are equal as we find a spot to park ourselves for the unalloyed bliss of a good day out.

The beach – where so much is lost and found.

Nobody, who has not been in the interior of a family, can say what the difficulties of any individual of that family may be.

JANE AUSTEN

I am the oldest of seven siblings who learned to squeeze ourselves into one pew at Mass, put 7 x 10 cents on the plate and, while pretending to pray virtuously, kept looking out for friends from similarly large families dragooned into Sunday worship by their parents. We were a family of faith, members of the Catholic tribe with its pride and particularities, doctrine and dogma, benedictions and blasphemies, certainties and contradictions, moral courage and sinfulness – a great, imperfect, inclusive, judgmental, erring human institution of two thousand years with its stained-glass stories of glory and eternal life and the central and abiding goodness of one man: Jesus of Nazareth.

Today, we are a family of different leanings. Life and its myriad lessons and experiences have challenged and changed us. We are a loving, supportive and motley collection who are now scattered around the country in Cairns, Brisbane, Bendigo and the suburbs of Melbourne. We are worlds away from the parochialism of those more innocent times. In today's secular, pluralist society, we are trying to be ordinary decent honest citizens whose actions are informed by compassion and justice. We are living out, more or less, the moral template left behind by our parents and the years of education in a system that prioritised loving God and loving neighbour. We are not virtue signalling or grievance afflicted, an urban elite or hamstrung by political correctness. We are siblings who love each other, put up with each other's idiosyncrasies and crazy passions and predilections, and know that we can be told the truth lovingly even if it hurts sometimes. As the Persian poet Rumi reminds us, 'We are all just walking each other home.' We are doing our best here and now with each other, with our wider families and with our friends.

My father was briefly disappointed when I married out. To a Protestant. I couldn't wait forever for the

Church's decision regarding an annulment, so we were married in a small country Presbyterian church by a pastor who had all the makings of a television evangelist. I wore a daffodil silk Laura Ashley dress and my flower girls carried sunflowers. Two and half years later, and with a three-month-old daughter, the annulment was approved, and we had a ratification ceremony conducted by dear old Father Brosnan, the man to whom Ronald Ryan gave his last confession. My husband and my father became good friends, spending many a Sunday afternoon robustly debating religious issues, with me presiding and intervening with placatory platitudes and cups of tea.

My parents' active faith gave the family a good foundation. A couple of us are still practising Catholics – trying to get it right. Others are more of the cultural brigade but still want the big Catholic events. One is not sure about it all because he is of a scientific-rational bent and another has done quite a lot of Buddhist formation. But our hearts still beat with those childhood lessons about kindness, sharing and the handing on and down of toys and clothes and books; looking out for those who did not share our good fortune and life chances.

There has been heartache, betrayal and sin in the larger family of faith, and many have understandably walked away from the Catholic Church. We were taught never to doubt Mother or Father; theirs was the word of God and we believed it. Fortunately for me, the religious sisters of my youthful education are still friends. Only last week I was out to lunch with one of these wonderful women. Almost fifty years have passed since she encouraged me as a gritty little Wing Attack in netball and put us through the integrated studies/themes approach to learning – the curriculum fad of the early 1970s. We were taught that God loved us, despite our small sins and failings; that his love was unconditional and everlasting. The Jesus I got to know as a child was my friend, not a wrathful avenging God, but someone I could talk to at the end of each day, who listened to my small prayers and ponderings.

My family memories are happy ones, but there are episodes of sadness that afflict all families. My mother suffered from depression for thirty years, underwent many ECT treatments, and although she loved us dearly, we could all be subjected to her sharp tongue which, on occasion, shrivelled our confidence. When she shone, she was a star and we were her seven little satellites. But she lost her equilibrium over the time and trial of looking after so many of us. She wore herself out with love. My father was devout and bookish, a writer of letters to priest and premiers, a quiet and persistent advocate for the unborn child. He was the deep anchor of the family.

I am a stepmother, but for a number of reasons, one of the boys has had little contact with us over the years. My daughter keeps the door ajar for the day that we meet again. In the wider family, there are separations and hurts and trying not to take sides and the disappointments of children not fulfilling their early promise. There are pockets of depression in our very normal family. We have our minor squabbles. We disagree about things. And occasionally we resort to shifting alliances, as is usual in big families where numbers count.

Fourteen years separate my birth from that of my youngest brother. We are a colourful bunch, with our various talents and temperaments and overlapping histories. There are stories that still surprise us. Only decades later did I learn that my purse was frequently raided by my younger at-school siblings, the missing coins purloined for sweet treats from the tuckshop. I never suspected a thing. I'm old enough to laugh at this belated confession of childhood pilfering and look back kindly at the nonchalance of my twenties where I had little idea where my money went. My younger brother tells me of the times I took him and his friends out to the Showgrounds or Moomba or treated him to a stay at one of my various rentals or share houses in North Fitzroy and Carlton. His memories still vivid, mine vague. In family, shared memories are sometimes recalled quite differently; one sibling's fabulous summer holiday in Castlemaine is another's interminable incarceration in the country.

The family unit of the past was revered as foundational to the workings of a functional society. It was the basis of identity and belonging, sometimes of title and property, more often of the working class before a bourgeoisie or middle class was invented. It was a small stronghold of affection and dependence in the turbulence of a wide and sometimes wild world. These days our families consist of blended configurations, the mixed marriage of different cultures, traditions and religions, the strange and strong tie of blood, the bond of common interests and worldviews, old friends who know your secrets and new friends who are trying to find them out, in-laws and out-laws and those who become family because they tagged on and stayed and became another permanent fixture at gatherings large and small. To me, family is not only about blood and genealogical kinship. It is also about where we are known and accepted and where we are at our most forgiven. We are not loved less because of a few missteps or the peccadilloes of personality that define us as different. In this wider, more inclusive definition of family, we can be our truest selves.

We celebrate anew the family circle of humanity in its infinite variety and endless difference, in its fierce and protective love and loyalty and its sometimes broken hearts.

The blessings of family are given to us the moment we take our first breath. They are with us till the last.

Family is bedrock and bosom.

It is home.

This is an edited version of an article previously published in *Australian Catholics*, Summer 2018.

Twenty years from now you will be more disappointed by the things you didn't do than by the ones you did do. So throw off the bowlines, sail away from the safe harbor. Catch the trade winds in your sails. Explore. Dream. Discover.

MARK TWAIN

We had always known about the picture because she had told us about it often enough, but as is the way with family stories, it had long been stored in the memory drive to be retrieved for later reference. So on my way to Paris, I thought I'd break my journey to spend one night in Bangkok. I would see for myself my

Aunt Valerie's painting; the painting that has adorned all the stationery and correspondence of the Oriental Hotel (now the Mandarin Oriental) since she painted the celebratory picture of its hundred years of genteel and gracious hospitality just over forty years ago.

On the hotel's centenary in 1976 she had been commissioned to paint a celebratory tribute to the original hotel from an old postcard. This was in the days of Anna Leonowens and the King of Siam and his entourage of wives and concubines and children. When the world map was splodged with colonial pink and Englishmen still thought they ruled the world. A bonus was that I'd get to mooch around the famous Author's Lounge and secretly wish that some of that literary alchemy would rub off on me. I could enjoy afternoon tea in an atrium bedecked with palms and white wicker chairs and starched linen tablecloths and see myself chatting urbanely to Somerset Maugham about the moon and sixpence and the travails of colonial life. The gentle incense of lemongrass would infuse the atmosphere and I'd swoon briefly over an expat life long gone.

My room had a great view over the Chao Phraya as I watched long barges sail slowly and small junks skip along the water, depositing and picking up tourists from the hotels lining the river. In my brown silk robe, I gazed into the high-rise distance of this busy metropolis and thought myself every bit a Thai princess. Reading an international paper at breakfast made me feel like a global citizen, somehow stepping me up and away briefly from my daily reality as a teacher in suburban Melbourne. I loved the rabble of elegant internationality as I helped myself to the smorgasbord and had three coffees because I didn't have to be anywhere for anyone. My dear husband had treated me to this rather expensive night away as he knew that I was pursuing more than just a picture in wanting to see this noted work.

In prior publications of *The Famous Hotels of the World* this special painting had been simply attributed to a contemporary artist. Now, we had managed to give my talented relative a bit more of a bio and credit where it was due. This was the woman whose life was lived out on the broad canvas of art and adventure. She had been evacuated from the Australian Legation in Cairo during the Suez Crisis and had been in Indo-China during that colonial war where she met Graham Greene; she a secretary who painted and he a foreign correspondent who would later turn this turbulent time into *The Quiet American*.

My aunt painted many members of the Thai Royal family, Harold Holt, soldiers and ambassadors, businessmen and surgeons, a papal secretary, friends and most of my family. The portraits of my parents are our own heirlooms; my father, the young doctor in white coat and stethoscope, and my mother, just married and looking regal in fur. In my bedroom I have a portrait of my grandmother (who died before I was born) and I often think of her and know of the love and support she gave her only daughter who would not be tamed into the conventional life expected of young women of the time. I see the portrait Valerie painted of me at twenty-one, true to life but somehow prettier than I ever remember being. Perhaps she saw the truth of my character, which is what the best portraitists do. She certainly got my eyes right. But looking at it now, I seem a bit experimental; my face not resolute enough, as if I haven't quite decided who I will be. In its oval gilt frame, perhaps it does look a little chocolate-boxy as she captures a certain youthful openness, the bloom of hope resident in a girl looking straight ahead, a girl as yet unfazed by any of the heartbreaks that life has in store. Perhaps my favourite aunt has dolled me up a little for posterity.

Valerie was an Archibald finalist in 1962 and exhibited in London with Sidney Nolan and Albert Tucker. She spoke excellent French (good German and Dutch, could get by comfortably in Italian and Spanish and could be understood in Thai and Arabic) and between painting portraits in Asia and Australia she used the portability of her excellent secretarial skills to find work in foreign affairs. Hers was a life of colour and occasional chaos. We affectionately called her a woman of mystery as she kept us guessing about much of what she did.

As I wandered through an exhibition of the Oriental's history, and burst into tears when I saw that she had been given her due, it was fascinating to see who had sojourned here. It was a list of movers and shakers; the rich, famous and powerful, the people who make history, the scions and scallywags, the great and the not-so-good. And it got me thinking about all those who weren't on the list – the behind-the-scenes fixers who make small things happen so that big things grab the headlines; the secretaries who keep the diary free or understand a certain gestural shorthand that helps take the ice out of a frosty diplomatic meeting; the woman whose work is not always on the books.

As I admired her painting, with its Impressionistic figures in long white dresses and open parasols promenading in the palm-treed garden outside the old hotel, I thought about her brush with so much real life; the travels of my aunt, Valerie O'Neill, and her story waiting to be told.

This is an edited version of an article previously published in *The Weekend Australian*, February 7–8 2015.

Breathe Paris in. It nourishes the soul.

VICTOR HUGO

The last time I saw Paris I was saying goodbye to love. That's why I was doing all those extra shifts at the Wimbledon Theatre, selling ice creams during matinees on my days off from my full-time job, doling out strawberry tubs to spoilt children and their spoilt mothers who didn't even bother to check their change. I was a red-pinnied usherette who smiled as the repertory companies did their big show in the city. I saw great character actors and hopeful drama graduates and soap opera B-list celebs past their use-by date. I saw David Essex and Donovan and any number of Christmas pantomimes featuring Cilla Black.

Living in London, I dieted on penury and feasted on promise – the promise of Paris in the springtime. The only way to close the curtain on a love story that was breaking my heart.

Thirteen years later, at the age of forty-eight, I again encounter this beautiful city. This time, I am in charge of my heart. It is safely at home in Melbourne with my husband and daughter, a heart that has been broken and fixed a couple of times, but has survived to a certain resilience, perhaps even a little carapace of toughness, because tender has so often meant tears. This time, I am a different woman. Not youngish and in love. Older and loved. Not held in the breathless embrace of co-dependence, a love that smothers and stifles, whose passion burns so hot that, as Cole Porter so memorably wrote, it just had to cool down.

This is the Paris of a woman of a certain age who is no longer flustered by the inattention of men. This is not to say that I have become some misbegotten hag. I still primp and preen and want to look good, but I don't worry about needlepoint criticism and the fact that my fashion sense is not quite *de rigueur*. At last, youth is no longer the only currency.

This time I bask in the hours of time to myself. No assignations or expectations. No clocking on or turning up. I spend an afternoon at the Opera House, shuffling along in awe, as I look at the vast resplendence around me. I wander slowly along dark corridors and find as I look above me a painting of a ballerina dressed in peacock feathers, her graceful hands outstretched above her plumage. I do not know her name, but she speaks to me, this back-wall beauty unremarked, archived from the rolling roistering thrum of modern life. I see Chagall's centrepiece – a riot of colour and playground simplicity, with its *joie de vivre* charmingly at odds with the serious seating of the boxes and the plush and gilded theatre.

Of course, I visit Sacré-Coeur and marvel at the view from the steps. This time, though, it has been desecrated. Protestors have daubed red paint on its ice-white birthday cake dome; ugly sacrilegious graffiti. This is a sore sight for eyes when I expect to see this triumphant prayer of architecture, when I expect to enter its portals for a quiet word with God and to catch my breath as I traverse the city on foot. Inside, it is so busy with people like me that I say a prayer in thanks for the man-made beauties of this city and the providence that enables me to be here on a perfectly ordinary, perfectly lovely day. Outside, I see a toy Eiffel Tower in the distance, floating in a diaphanous shimmer of sunshine and pollution.

One afternoon I leave my tour group so I can pop into Notre Dame and say a prayer for the just-deceased Pope John Paul II. Thousands of others are doing the same. Later, I wander happily through the streets and alleyways of the Marais. My French is schoolgirl at best, but I attempt to purchase postcards and trinkets without giving into English at the first grimace from the vendor.

I stumble across a picture restorer's shop and curiosity beckons me inside. There are dark pictures of the suffering Christ on the cross and bucolic Impressionistic scenes of families by a river and down the back are art school mistakes. Just as I am about to leave, I spy a canvas. It is an impression of a river with a church in the background painted in hues of blue, green and grey. I like to think it is the back view of Notre Dame with the ribbon of the Seine floating past, its thousands of years of sworn secrets never to be unlocked by those who would write her history.

I ask the *vendeuse*, who is also the restorer, its price. And amazingly, I can afford it. It's not signed, but it's original and it's not one of those awful daubings that is more tart than art. I don't think it is an art school mistake. It is a proper postcard from Paris, one that once I have it cleaned and framed properly, will adorn my walls, an abiding memory of this most alluring of cities that so captured, and broke, my heart thirteen years ago.

A walk about Paris will provide lessons in history, beauty, and in the point of Life.

THOMAS JEFFERSON

It's a drizzly morning in an otherwise summery Paris as I run through the leafy convent garden to Mass in the beautiful nineteenth century Gothic chapel. Naturally, the liturgy is in French and I recognise *Père, Fils et Saint Esprit, le Seigneur, paix*, and of course, *Amen*. Much is lost in translation as I pick up the odd word that has somehow been retrieved from my long distant secondary school French. The gathered sisters of various ages and nationalities sing hymns that carry high above to linger momentarily as tiny motes with notes. I am surrounded by statues and stained-glass windows and the silence after everyone leaves is gloomily expansive. Next door is a busy hospital, but behind these anonymous high walls the peace is not breached, except for the distant hum of traffic. I am a world away from my real life. I have briefly slipped the bonds of duty and expectation and dishes and corrections at night. Somehow, in the lovely cosmic enlargement of heart that comes from simply being happy, I am at home in the world.

I am staying in a modest hostel in the seventh arrondissement. Not far from the Boulevard St Jacques, the chapel appears to be a secret, except to the community, a few wayfaring pilgrims, the odd missionary and small troops of school students. I have a clean and simple room and sleep like a queen. I slurp coffee out of a bowl for breakfast and crunch hungrily into a baguette slathered with butter and strawberry jam. For dinner, I find a local grocer and discover a crème brûlée that cancels out the good intentions of apples and yoghurt. I walk quickly past a group of young men with snarly slavering dogs, scuttling like a *grand-mère* who is late home. During the day, avoiding the obvious places, I walk around with my head up, looking about me, enchanted by the residential aesthetic where homes have art deco sculptures on facades or garlanded cherubs astride entrances or old cast iron door knockers that serve as security. I visit suburban churches and local galleries and find that wandering is a wonderful way to stumble across unexpected gems that make the mundane sparkle, thrilling in their momentary narrative, evanescent as clouds. I am looking for the small and delightful, little intimacies that lift the heart; the cat basking in the stripes of sun on a window shelf, the glimpse of a beautiful painting in an old gold frame in a family apartment, the secret garden hidden behind large nineteenth century oak doors, the quick step of poise and purpose of sleek young Parisians.

Out of my third-floor shuttered window I look onto the white dome of the Observatoire and I am but a fifteen-minute stroll from the geometric grace of the Luxembourg Gardens. Here, I commandeer one of the green chairs and settle down to enjoy the promenade. I watch as children play with toy boats on the octagonal Grand Bassin pond, chic elderly ladies walk dogs, enamoured couples canoodle, businessmen talk urgently into their phones, teenagers take selfies and joggers keep one foot in front of the other. All the while, everyone keeps off the grass.

What joy to watch *tout le monde* and bask in good weather, to gather my usually splintered thoughts and to revel in the generous gift of time. The goldfish in the Medici Fountain glide unperturbed in their watery fiefdom and the statues gaze blindly. I notice the sharper blue of the northern sky and the dappled green of clean-cut topiary and the perfection of palm trees that look like props. I feel as if I have wandered into an Impressionist painting. I could be one of Seurat's *flâneuses*, picked out in bright daubs, enjoying the warmth on my skin and feeling some sedate *joie de vivre*.

Each time I have visited Paris I have been a different person: secondary school friend of long-legged medical student keen on Napoleonic history; university friend of a female surgeon who is generous with her much larger budget; long-term girlfriend who is about to have her heart broken; laughing old friend who remembers the fun and friendships of those tender teenage years; slightly more solid and sartorially colourful married older pilgrim who is finally meeting herself with a degree of acceptance, but not quite *je ne regrette rien*.

Each time I have become more enamoured of her secret ways, away from the tide of tourists and the half hour stop at souvenir shops. Each time the city of light has offered me a different aspect of her personality: coquette, aesthete, intellectual, mime artist, chameleon. For me, Paris is a city of a thousand possible sliding-door selves. I wonder which version of me I'll find wandering and wondering in the Paris of my reinvention next time.

*Life, like a dome of many coloured glass,
stains the white radiance of eternity.*

PERCY BYSSHE SHELLEY

I have often remarked to friends that my holidays sometimes feel like a stained-glass blur as colours merge into a kaleidoscopic and aesthetic overload. My head spins as I gaze happily at all sorts of saintly narratives. It could be Chartres or York or Sainte-Chapelle, or an earnest Norman chapel. More often than not, it is a small village church at the end of a country lane that beckons me to light a candle, say a prayer and bide awhile as I wander along the aisle and marvel at some delicate feature of woodwork or brass or a window hidden in the gloom behind the altar. I am transported by both the luminosity of the work and the great devotional efforts of often unsung artisans. It might be a spectacular rose window or a small window in a reliquary, an ancient roundel or the tinted glow of a lozenge of light paid for by a benefactor for departed loved ones. I think my grandmother must be to blame – all those afternoons spent in the beautiful Ladye Chapel at St Francis' in Melbourne lighting candles and repenting of my very tiny venial sins.

Some of my favourite stained-glass windows are in modest parish churches. In the Church of St Mary the Virgin in Swanage, England, there are martial windows with medieval saints emboldened in armour. The one that took my fancy was of Saint Francis of Assisi gambolling among the animals. In the middle of France, in the small village of Parassy, is an unadorned barn-shaped church where there is a wonderful rendering of a young Jeanne d'Arc as a simple peasant girl, long before voices and visions transformed her into the Maid of Orleans.

Edmundsbury Cathedral in Bury St Edmunds provides awe and delight with its wonderful Creation Window. Its upper lights are full of knights and heraldry and below are scenes from the Genesis story. I see Eve and her silk-spun auburn tresses and the gorgeous detail of the multiplication of birds, etched on white glass feathered against geometric panels of cobalt blue and purple. Anyone gazing at this window must surely be appreciative of the artistry here that tells the founding story of Judeo-Christian belief in such lush colour. It is an invitation to enter the numinous and to be affected and uplifted by the splendour in the glass.

In Boston, I have planned to visit the Arlington Street Church and its beautiful Tiffany windows. I am dragging my brother and sister along and part of our travel deal is that we'll indulge each other. This is my morning. We've walked from Boston Common and I note the bronze statue of Tadeus Kosciuszko, after whom our highest Australian mountain is named, located in the public gardens just near the church building. We wonder why he is celebrated here on a modest corner of the city, and only later, after doing a bit of research (Googling, really), do we understand just what a hero this celebrated Pole was. I love that these incidental sightings, of statues and paintings and odd buildings or unusual plaques which are generally unheralded, can lead you to find out so much more. It is said knowledge is power, but it is also the source of other gratifications when new things are discovered or made known. It also suggests that we need to keep looking up and around and about so that we do not miss the small and delightful ornamentations that can be lost when something grand devours all the acclaim.

Apart from gazing at the beauty and craftsmanship of the windows, we can also touch the glass and feel the texture. This is unusual as often such windows have that 'Do Not Touch' aura about them or are completely out of reach in the spaciousness of vast Gothic interiors. I marvel at how the artisans could swirl the colours into such luminescence. Molten drapery glass was twisted with metal tongs as it came through the rollers to replicate the folds of clothing. This creates an almost 3D effect and brings the windows to life with their subtle sculpted mounds and clefts. Part of the allure of these windows is this tactile topography which clearly shows the textural deliberation of their making.

In the creation of works from the Tiffany Studio, confetti glass, tissue-thin glass upon glass of different colours, creates the signature diaphanous blooms of blossom and lily and verdant foliage seen so often in their famous lamps. Here at the Arlington Street Church is a softer pastel palette that highlights a milky opalescent effect, whilst using reds, blues and greens for accents. The borders at this church are art nouveau in style, using acanthus leaf scrolls, flowers and vines as a framework for the larger visual narrative.

Designed by Tiffany's chief designer of ecclesiastical windows, Frederic Wilson, the Arlington windows present scenes from the life of Jesus of Nazareth and sayings from the Beatitudes. I love the angels with their protective mother-of-pearl wings. They are vigilant and not too ethereal. Neither obviously male nor female, they are the guardian companions of the light. John the Baptist exudes a square-jawed frontiersman strength and heroism as he sits near reeds representing the Sea of Galilee. The sky behind him appears almost Impressionistic with its vaporous blue tinged with pink and orange, a celestial background that is beautiful to behold. In an unusual scene from the Bible stories, Mary enfolds her twelve-year-old son whom she had thought lost in the Temple. A menorah in the background indicates that this is a sacred place for the Hebrew people. This is a mother and child moment of great humanity because we know what it is to hug a child tightly, fiercely, when they have been lost and later found.

The seventeenth century poet George Herbert wrote in 'The Elixir':

> A man that looks on glass
> On it may stay his eye
> Or if he pleaseth, though it pass,
> And then the heav'n espy.

This is an invitation to gaze at stained-glass windows, and through them access a story of faith. It may only be a brief encounter, but it still resonates in the heart of the viewer long after they have left the church. One can be entranced by the small thoughtful detail, the artist's intimacy with his subject on display. This vibrant complementarity of picture and colour speaks to my soul.

It is not a stained-glass blur. It is a benediction.

As the light is diffused through these timeless Tiffany windows they take on a lustrous crystalline glow.

They really are heavenly.

*It's not what you look at that matters,
it's what you see.*

HENRY DAVID THOREAU

My first understanding of the link between religion and art came as a child. In one of the long corridors of my convent school there was a nineteenth century copy of Raphael's *The Sistine Madonna*. Mary, on a cushion of cloud, cuddled her Christ child while the pretty putti (seen these days on everything from stationery to home wares) seemed to lean impishly out of the bottom of the canvas. Gazing up at her were Saint Sixtus and Saint Barbara and in the left-hand corner was the pope's mitre. On the opposite wall, Saint Michael was vanquishing the devil. Feet encased in medieval blue thongs, he raised his silver sword menacingly and the whole picture was shrouded in a sort of Gothic gloom. The story of faith further unfolded around me through holy picture prayer cards, plaster cast statues, my grandmother's print of Ferruzzi's late Victorian *Madonnina* and the exquisite Italian brass reliefs of the Stations of the Cross in the school chapel. The well-thumbed *The Little Picture Book of Saints* was almost as important as the learnt-by-heart green catechism in knowing the who's who of the heavenly realm.

For me, a singular joy is spending a couple of unhurried hours at the NGV and looking at old favourites and then noticing something new. It might be a splash of colour in the gloom, a tree decorated with the softest blossom, the small smile of one of John Brack's hurrying pedestrians or the intricate rendering of lace on a cuff. I love the work of Emmanuel Philips Fox and his bucolic scenes of family life: a child with a hoop in the midst of a family garden party, the painting rendered with the lightness and charm of a picture-book idyll. I reconsider with delight the work of the Heidelberg School, now known less parochially as Australian Impressionism. The familiar is suddenly revitalised; the old story re-emerging with a new twist.

This is especially so when we view great works of religious art at firsthand. There is nothing so moving as seeing a painting alive in its own flesh, the canvas on which daubs and gouts and smooth strokes and varnishing and brilliance are seen up close and personal. This story is never exhausted. It is reread by everyone who looks up in the Sistine Chapel or sees the sculpted marble folds of *La Pièta*, everyone who looks at Byzantine mosaics or rejoices in the stained-glass beauty of Sainte-Chappelle. It is seen in the carving of a wooden crucifix or the chasing of fine gold on a medieval chalice. It is the beauty abundant in churches, synagogues, temples, mosques and shrines – mankind's artistry in response to the awe and wonder of the transcendent.

The response to art, in all its forms, starts in the heart. It is modified by aesthetics and personal preference. Some art lovers swoon over sculptures or icons or Flemish diptychs. Some love ceramics or illuminated manuscripts or the works of El Greco. Some love what the newer arts offer in the forms of digital technology and installations. What art gives us is the opportunity to respond authentically to what speaks to us in our lives. And it doesn't matter whether one's taste is conservative or adventurous, well-informed or intuitive, whether one is a connoisseur or just likes what they see. If the artwork moves you beyond yourself, it has done its job.

The beauty of art is that it tells us the stories of ourselves in great whirlpools of wonder, in a cornucopian creativity that invites us to look closely. These stories may be strictly historical, grandly mythological, religiously instructive or drawn from an imagination that can somehow bejewel a small domestic moment and give it a universality of meaning. These narratives or tableaux are time capsule moments; frozen at the time of completion, but still speaking to us across the years. Like time capsules, sometimes there are felicitous discoveries or unusual finds or the sudden and urgent poignancy that we share because we have accessed a life caught at a certain intersection of history. This life, caught on canvas, pivots between the global and the personal, and we understand it because we share it.

I share something with the woman who gazed at a Titian two centuries ago and with what my great-great grandchildren will see in that same resplendent work. This is one of the miracles of human existence. The story starts before us. We have a small role played out on the bank and shoal of our own time, and the narrative continues. That's why I love those places where others have stood or prayed or played or laughed or loved before me – churches, galleries, museums, theatres, libraries and grand public parks; all of them celebrating the human story and inviting the past to mingle with the present.

We look at depictions of the life and death of Jesus of Nazareth, of saints and sinners, popes and peasants, of the aristocratic gentleman and the unknown female and we eavesdrop on what has brought us this far. We all know of the treasures of the Vatican and the marvels of Florence, of Da Vinci's *The Last Supper* or Rembrandt's *The Prodigal Son*. But visit any church in Europe and religious art in all its glorious and glorifying forms are on display. In small local churches there are canvases and frescoes, altarpieces and tapestries, reliquaries and statues, ornate pulpits and baptismal fonts, engraved and gilded chalices and sculpted cherubim cavorting. The interior of the Benedictine Abbey in the small Swiss town of Engelberg has to be seen to be believed. The paintings and frescoes are beautiful. Perhaps they transfixed me the more so because I felt the hand of faith behind them; to translate the story of the Assumption so beautifully, surely there must have been conviction in the heart of the artist. In a shameless tourist snap on a trip to the Vatican, I am seen clasping one of the giant Baroque cherubs holding the holy water font near the entrance to St Peter's Basilica, almost caressing the centuries old marble, star-struck in the face of such beauty and workmanship. And everywhere there is the glory of stained glass, telling its transparent story in reds and blues and rose windows in the great cathedrals, like Amiens or Cologne, and in the small parish churches of the far-flung faithful.

The artist tells the story in their own way, with their own imaginative and interpretative licence, whilst staying true to the original narrative. Michelangelo is reputed to have said that he was setting free the angel inside a block of marble he intended to carve. This is what artists do – they set free their creation and its beauty can be the means of opening the heart to prayer or meditation. The artist has been able to transcend the merely pictorial and produce a work that is inspired or visionary. They are compelled to release their new telling of an old story.

Vincent van Gogh wrote that when he needed religion, all he had to do was gaze at the stars and paint. He wrote to his brother Theo in 1882 that 'one must work long and hard to arrive at the truthful'. Great art leads us to truth, and it is often the work of years, of blood, sweat and tears, of agony and ecstasy, of a heart and talent that cannot be gainsaid. The truth must out.

When I gaze at the great works of art, whether religious or not, my first prayer is to be thankful for the gifts of all artists; for the canvas on which their talent comes to life in colour and brushstroke, in detail and depth, in the hymn of truth and beauty redolent in their artistic vision. I marvel at the human capacity for invention and narrative in works that take me beyond myself. I am enchanted by the soft shimmering suggestion of gold on a tree as the day dips into dusky evening, the Madonna's look of love for her holy child and the blue-veined hand of an elderly scholar grasping a vellum-bound book. I have my favourite paintings which give me the joy of looking and looking again: John Singer Sargent's *Carnation, Lily, Lily, Rose* in the Tate Gallery; *La Japonaise*, a portrait of Monet's first wife Camille in a kimono at the Boston Museum of Fine Arts. I thank God that I have the gift of appreciation and reverence, the ability to acknowledge with humility that I am in the company of greatness and that this is a gift for all time in the rich and enduring telling of the human story.

This is an edited version of an article previously published in *Australian Catholics*, Summer 2013.

*If the only prayer you ever said is Thank You,
that would be enough.*

MEISTER ECKHART

Rosslyn Chapel came to worldwide attention in the film *The Da Vinci Code* where it was a place of secrets and codes and supposed messianic DNA. But on a blustery Edinburgh morning, with the sky crouching grey and low, it becomes the focal point of history lovers, Dan Brown acolytes and the odd holidaying family pausing on their way to the Highlands.

What delights me is the fluid and decorative mix of Christian and pagan motifs. The hundred or so green men with their gargoyle visages emerge from the stonework to stare blindly ahead, the legacy of a church built in the fifteenth century. This contrasts with the high Victoriana exemplified by the stained-glass windows. The human drama of the building is also recorded for posterity. Just as Notre Dame in Paris has its Quasimodo face gazing over the demi-monde, so too in Rosslyn, in a corner near the entrance, is the eternally ugly face of a jealous master mason who killed his gifted young apprentice. Elsewhere, the carving of an angel playing the bagpipes adds an appropriate local motif amongst the stories told in stone.

On the day we visit, there is a midday prayer service and all visitors are invited to pause and pray. Tourist talk stops and the two young female stonemasons put aside the chisels they are using to restore the stonework. The chaplain reminds us of the importance of attention as we briefly reclaim the silence. My prayers are the same ones I would say in Melbourne, but I love that I am saying them in this special place of worship that has witnessed the faith of crusader Knights Templar and titled families, of villagers and visitors, of the virtuous and the venal. I sit with the spirits of saints and sinners and ask for mercy.

Over the past few months I have walked carefully around tombs embedded in uneven church floors, their inscriptions barely legible as time takes its toll. I have ventured down into cold and clammy crypts. Stone cold is a sort of spectral shivering of mould and moist and tormented souls. I have seen ruined abbeys and monasteries and signed the visitors' book in spare and spacious redundant churches because they no longer have the people to form a congregation. They have been deconsecrated into community centres; the secular impulse having the last word on the sacred. I have seen great works of devotional art and lit numerous candles; little flickers of flame briefly ardent as they have whisked my earthbound longings to a higher plane.

In every church I have visited, I have imagined those who have come before me and knelt in the same pew – a motley collection of Christians in a continuum of distracted worship, their long-ago prayers still extant in the ether despite the depredations of time and demography. I wonder whether here at Rosslyn a careworn peasant woman clad in her clan tartan uttered an urgent mother's prayer for her sons as they went to war? Did a lonely widower mourn his wife of many years and dream of meeting her again at heaven's gate? Were scallywag urchins making faces during tedious homilies and did a bonnie young lass's swain wink at her as she blushed modestly? The priests may have been charmingly articulate or blustery and gruff, all intent, in their own way, on saving souls. Perhaps they glanced at the pew and noticed a certain absence, or a renewed attendance, because they knew of the family's travails and honoured the inviolability of the seal of confession. Was my pew reserved for the St Clair family on whose estate the chapel has stood since the fifteenth century? Perhaps a local landowner had secured a sort of ownership by dint of sitting in the same pew over generations of worship and no-one dared to suggest he sit elsewhere. Then, as now, kneeling and standing and kneeling again in a sort of liturgical dance was fine for the young and spry, but not for the aged bodies of the old poacher, the erudite Edinburgher or the devout sway-backed women who worked the kitchen on the estate and lived in a small bothy.

Over the centuries, the flavours of faith practised in the chapel have changed; once staunchly Catholic, now the Episcopalian Church of Scotland and with an historic thread of Freemasonry to add to its feel of mystery. And with its recent secular celebrity, it is a place for all who visit, of any faith or none, to pause and ponder. Still, the heartfelt petitions from those in the pews have remained constant over the centuries as they have prayed through lives that have been both bruised and blessed. Congregants have sunk into Rosslyn's ancient pews for generations, glad of the respite from hard labour in the fields and farms, entranced by the stained-glass windows and the visual clues carved deeply in stone around them. In surges of desperation and devotion, they have prayed with broken hearts and spirits sore, in the hope of being heard.

At lovely Rosslyn Chapel under a lowering Scottish sky, I thank God for the joys and discoveries of travelling and seeing in chapels and cathedrals, in great cities and tiny hamlets, the handiwork in stone and glass and wood of the unsung artisans and craftsmen whose work stands, mute but in glorious testament, centuries later.

Educating the mind without educating the heart is no education at all.

ARISTOTLE

Back in the mid-70s the nuns thought that I was a possible candidate for a vocation. Perhaps they recognised something in my adolescent yearnings, in my way of being in the world that had prompted them to think of me as a fit for that special consecrated life. But I was eighteen and life held other meanings for me. Temporal temptations and opportunities took hold, and the appeal of a vocation was readily displaced by the urgencies of new friends, a new independence and the fun and games of the Law Revue at Melbourne University.

Almost forty years later I am now working with these same nuns at my *alma mater* and despite my strange and circuitous career trajectory, my nomadic travels, my benignly neglectful and lovingly indulgent motherhood, my delight in words and writing and my daily work as an educator, somehow the circle of vocation is being completed within me. I am now fulfilling that universal call to holiness, using (I like to think) my gifts wisely and well. I have deliberately chosen to work in the Catholic system because, as well as the joys of teaching English, I want to pass on some of the joys of faith. To date, I have had the great privilege of working with the Good Samaritans and the Dominicans and now am at home with the charism of my childhood years, that of the Faithful Companions of Jesus. I am fulfilling what Meister Eckhart remarked of when he said that the vocation is found when one is finally back in the house they had never left.

My educational philosophy is born of my own experience. I had wonderful teachers and my school days were happy. The teachers knew their subject and they knew me. I was named and known. I was marvellously encouraged with fair-minded feedback that enabled me to improve and to see myself as someone who could do well if I worked hard. Together with the academic rigours of school life, there was always the sacred tapestry being woven into my soul. The Catholic mould was set quite firmly and I embraced it all with a glad heart and open and unquestioning ways. I was a biddable student, perhaps something of a teacher pleaser, but I knew my prayers and my catechism. I loved the romance of the dusky chapel with its flickering votive candles, its gladioli floral offerings, its beeswaxed pews, fug of incense and hushed gloom.

The golden tabernacle was the centre point of worship as we trooped in to say our prayers. I loved the hymns, processions, statues, saints' days and the treats from Reverend Mother on her birthday as we curtsied to her and presented floral tributes. I loved the pictures of Our Lady and the made-up stories about the black-habited nuns and the parts of the convent that were out of bounds behind heavy oak doors. I loved the dash of mystery as we talked about saints and spectres and the Grey Lady who reputedly stalked the corridors at night.

The colour of my faith was a happy one and the religious education of my younger years did not make me fearful or guilty, but joyful. There may have been venial sins but I didn't dwell on them for too long. I was a regular at confession, said grace before meals, attended Mass, sang with the guitar group at the youth mass, 'Walked Against Want' and made friends who were Baptists.

I was, and I am, happy to be Catholic. I am at home in my faith – it is the cloak I wear, not invisible, not haute couture, but wrapping me in a warmth, its warp and weft inextricably entwined in the skein of the sacred knitted into my soul. Now in the ripeness of my middle years, I am recognising that I am fulfilling a calling, a destiny, where my faith and life are synergistically aligned in a workplace that enables me to do God's work and a good day's work. This is not to say that I am suddenly softly saintly, nor am I becalmed in mid-career, but I am simply in service as a team player, with the occasional original idea, a chortle in the staffroom, the odd whinge, but mostly the satisfactions of doing something daily with the best of my being.

I am of the wholehearted belief that we, as educators in life and faith, in Maths and English, in core curriculum discoveries and non-timetabled delights, do write on the souls of the next generation. As an educator, I believe that I am doing good, and often a good that will not be seen in KPIs or objective outcomes or external benchmarks or reportable on an end-of-semester report, a good that flowers in character and attitude and ultimately in behaviour.

I am in the right job for my disposition and talents and I have a creative licence to cover the curriculum in my own way. There is a singular joy in receiving an inspired piece of student writing or hearing a heartfelt prayer in homeroom. It is inspiring – and strange – to think that my lesson on apostrophes may be remembered because I used humour or poetry to illustrate my point. Sometimes I joke to my students that they may reminisce at their forty-year reunion about that teacher in Year 7 – what was her name? – who talked a lot, explained big words, edited their writing for student publication, whose favourite mantra was 'quality, not quantity', and who had a fine disregard for the teacher dress code.

How fortunate I am that my personal and professional passions are aligned. I love words and what they can do to improve the world; how they can enable conversation and dialogue and critique and healthy and respectful dissent. I love that we can contribute to conversations in the public square; that our letters to the editor, or comments on a moderated website or pithy one-liners in the paper can contribute, sometimes passionately or poignantly or with humour, to an issue concerning the wider community. This is the *vox populi*. I tell my students that this is the place to voice an opinion, share a thought, contribute meaningfully to debate so that we are all improved. It is the place for civil, not coarse, discourse.

I have a faith I want to share – not dogmatically, but invitationally, so that my students have hope and a framework for their own good work in the world. I am happy to share stories and insights and frame the existential questions that are part of the journey we all share. I can answer the tricky moral questions sensitively, mindful of the balance between personal and professional. I know that teenagers want to check my standing on an issue as they continue to build their own moral compass. In an age where a tsunami of information and the smorgasbord of choice can overwhelm, sometimes it's just the quiet thoughtful word that can help in the profound formation of the young adult.

I am at home in my working life and teaching is my charism. I have my moments of transcendence when I know God is giving me a nod of approval in my work. I am of service. I can share my gifts. I can tell stories and laugh and encourage and listen. I can kindle a passion for learning in others. I can join them in the pursuit of something that will last beyond us. And even on those days when lessons are dull and my performance is below par there is still some good being done, unseen, in the way I can choreograph a climate of hope in my class.

Saint John Henry Newman wrote that God had committed him to some work to which he had committed no other, that he was a link in a chain, a bond of connection between persons. That is where I am today, a link in the chain of the Catholic tradition and continuum. I have been called to do what I can with what I have. My calling is to engage those young people around me, just as I was engaged half a lifetime ago, so that they too can arrive at that moment of recognition, when they acknowledge that they are finally fulfilling the life that God dreamed for them.

Education is simply the soul of a society as it passes from one generation to another.

GILBERT KEITH CHESTERTON

I loved school. In particular, I loved my school, the school that saw me through from six-year-old Prep to eighteen-year-old-prefect. This was one of the places I learned to be me, to make lifelong friends, to build my faith, to believe that the world was waiting for me to take my place in it. Today, after a late arrival to teaching via a colourful and circuitous career path, I have the privilege of teaching in some of those same classrooms, now refurbished brightly without teacher platforms and chalky blackboards and desks with blackened inkwells.

Some might argue that returning to one's *alma mater* is an unadventurous and lacklustre choice – a going backwards into the comfort zone of the known. For me, however, it was the opportunity to offer something back to the school that had nurtured me. I saw the advertisement in *The Age* and applied because my heart has always been with the good women who taught me. It didn't hurt that my daughter was already at the school and that I was a member of the parent rock 'n' roll band, The deGENerates. We played fundraisers at the school, at golf clubs and reception centres and church halls, at birthdays, parties, anything, all of us liking a bit of centre-stage attention and applause for a good cause. My references checked out. I passed the interview, lacing it with some pedagogical puffery and a bit of gravitas, and I got the job.

I now teach in those classrooms of the past; those classrooms where the teachers knew me and taught expertly and without the need for assistive technology that, it seems to me, can effectively disguise a student's knowledge or ability. An interactive whiteboard is there for those teachers who like some colour and movement and who have been seduced by the purported wizardry of such technology. I am old-school enough to whip out my marker immediately when I wish to add to the board, no fiddle-faddling with projectors and codes and wiring and dropping out. I am old-school enough to be able to teach if technology fails. I am old-school enough not to need Grammarly!

I still possess my Form 3 essays on *To Kill a Mockingbird*, written in a large round hand and spattered with the teenage polysyllabic sludge of trying too hard to impress. I have never forgotten those southern belles soft as frosted teacakes. I had the good fortune to have a wonderful teacher, Miss Hiatt, who gently reminded me that fewer and better words make for a good essay. Forty years later, my daughter also got to know Atticus, Scout and Jem Finch and the valuable lesson of walking in someone else's skin as she hurried up the same long corridors to class. In the early 2020s, the novel is again on the curriculum, paired with that other classic, the film version of *Twelve Angry Men* where Henry Fonda as Juror 8 pleads for the life of a troubled Hispanic boy by suggesting there is reasonable doubt as to his guilt. What a joy to be able to analyse these works and look into the workings, good and bad, of the human heart.

Yes, the classics are classics for a reason.

One of the mantras of my Melbourne convent education at Genazzano in the 60s and 70s was the universal and scary phrase 'learning by heart'. We learnt times tables by heart, poems by heart, the names of planets and river systems and capitals and historic dates by heart. Most especially we learnt our spelling lists by heart because we had a test every week and personal mortification for me was a shoddy nineteen out of twenty. I learned by heart the answers to my catechism questions and recited them piously and not merely for the reward of a holy picture which could be swapped on the asphalt at playtime. Learning by heart meant that we spent the time doing something properly and well and although there were times when memory failed, or performance anxiety clouded our recitation, there was also a satisfaction in being able to understand and retain facts and figures and carry in our minds some of the glories of the language.

Learning by heart has another meaning which has more resonance than the ability to recall the wives of Henry VIII in correct order, beheadings and all. Although we didn't know it at the time, we were learning by heart to be our best selves, to be considerate of others, to belong to a class and school community. Through the years of our schooling we were learning in our wilful, untutored, open, childish hearts to be a friend in need and in deed.

Learning by heart was very much at the core of the curriculum as the teachers, religious and lay, took the time to really know us. I was always known and named; a little bit teacher's pet because I cleaned the blackboards and joined in and knew more than my prayers. I was encouraged and affirmed and liked and I learned to like myself and like others. My school endeavoured to write on the souls of the next generation, to enlarge the potential of each child so they found purpose and meaning and their own unique place in the world.

I was awakened to much in the world around me by those who taught and loved me. They gave me tiny fragments of their hearts when they smiled at me or patted me on the shoulder or cheered me on as I ran third in the two hundred metres. They made me feel good about myself and that being part of something, like a team or a House or a choir, was important. They applauded when I was on stage, trying to make something of my minor role. They encouraged my wordy student efforts in the school magazine. They unleashed in me the curiosity of finding out more, of reading widely, of experimenting with words and ideas, of performing, of putting in, of being cheerful and willing, of looking ahead with hope.

It has been written that children may forget what a teacher said, but they will never forget how that teacher made them feel. Learning by heart is not something that can be timetabled, but it is a lesson that is easily taught, and caught.

Learning by heart matters because it teaches us that the real lesson of life is love.

Every saint has a bee in his halo.

ELBERT HUBBARD

My childhood piety was of the unquestioning kind, seasoned by the rhythm of the rosary, the regular confession of venial sins and the stories of the saints. These sainted lives became the fabric of a faith peopled by the mysterious, the martyred and the mystical. My mother possessed a tiny silver-encased relic of Saint Maria Goretti, the patron saint of girls, and I would gaze at it with a mixture of curiosity and alarm, drawn into another realm of story, worlds away from Dick and Jane and the adventures of the Secret Seven.

At school we would walk across to the grotto where Our Lady stood in mystical visitation in front of the young Bernadette. We would then proceed to the chapel where the flicker of votive candles and the potent swirl of incense and imagination fuelled my wonderment. I came to understand the concept of the Trinity by hearing of Saint Patrick's use of the shamrock as a teaching tool and could even see him with his shillelagh as his staff as he converted pagans. I couldn't name the numinous, but it was all around me as the nuns taught me about the men and women whose lives were committed to God.

Our supplication to the saints depended on their stories. And the grislier the better. There was no room for the neat deaths of gentle expiration or graced last moments or celestial dormition. The stories of scourging and gouging and lions' dens and glorious unbowed, unflinching martyrdom took hold. This was faith of the lion-hearted variety. I loved it from the safety of my own unchallenged freedom to believe. I still have a copy of *Miniature Stories of the Saints (Volume 4)* held together with sticky tape and hope, its pages well-thumbed over the years. First published in 1946 by the Rev Daniel A. Lord, SJ, these small books still sell well in parish porches, a sort of *Golden Book* for the saints. As a little girl I was rather taken with modest Saint Zita, the patron saint of servants, who didn't have the provenance of Queen Clotilde, wife of Clovis, or Catherine of Siena, Doctor of the Church and one of twenty-three children.

Some saints cover a lot of holy ground. My mother was devoted to Saint Gerard Majella, the patron saint of expectant mothers. Saint Anthony, as the patron saint of lost things, has many calls on him, for missing keys and misplaced credit cards. I wonder if sometimes there is not the odd Catholic who prays to Saint Anthony because they feel, in a world that is so demand-driven, they have lost their mind. We now have our own home-grown Saint Mary of the Cross MacKillop, a girl born in Melbourne who died in Sydney and knew that poverty of the soul started with the poverty of the streets. It was she who taught in a humble classroom, who founded an order of nuns who understood the drover and the cockie, the harried wife and the homeless man. It was she who understood that things needed to be done and did them in her no-nonsense, sleeves-rolled-up, practical Australian way. It was she who recognised that 'we are but travellers here', as is inscribed on her tomb.

I love the fact that there are patron saints for practically everything. Saint Crispin is the patron saint of bikies, and leatherworkers, tanners and cobblers. Saint Drogo is the patron saint of coffee houses. And then there are the saints of early times with names such as Symphorianus, Zeno and Gwinear. And I was fascinated to find out that the phrase 'the bonfire of the vanities' originated from Saint Bernardino of Siena, a popular fifteenth century preacher who encouraged his flock to burn objects of temptation or material vanities. Apiarists have Saint Ambrose and lawyers have Saint Thomas More and undertakers have Joseph of

Arimathea, the righteous man who provided the burial tomb for Jesus. And for all those whose computers have crashed or whose work has been lost in cyberspace we now have Saint Isidore, the patron saint of technology and the internet, to whom desperate invocations may be made at any hour of the day or night, anywhere on Earth – truly a universal saint for the twenty-first century globally connected village.

Dear Saint Christopher, beloved of travellers, and to whom we dedicated many a family car trip on the slow Sundays of the past, has since been delisted by the Vatican, but he still holds a place in popular imagination.

Much of my childhood faith was learned through my grandmother who would often respond with the phrases 'Saints alive' or 'Saints preserve us' or 'Jesus, Mary and Joseph' when her usually inexhaustible patience had been sorely tried. She really did have the patience of a saint. Now, in my middle years, the saints are as alive to me as they ever were. This special Catholic cavalcade makes me marvel at the downright goodness and charity and perseverance of those who put God and goodness first, often at great personal cost. Pope Francis has recently said that we all have the capacity for saintliness, although I think the inner sinner is often the winner.

Saint Paul in his Letters often greeted the early Christians as saints as they went about their ordinary lives. If we choose to, we can be one of those everyday saints who do our best wherever we find ourselves. We might not make it to the big list of the canonised or the beatified or the heroic – the saint, blessed or venerable – but we will have done a little of God's good work in our own small spheres.

We can be – *Saints alive*!

Youth's sway and youth's play,
of songs and flowers and love ...

DANTE GABRIEL ROSSETTI

In 1973 I watched (with a billion and a half others) as Elvis beamed into my life. It was *Aloha from Hawaii* and I watched in awe, a fifteen-year-old Melbourne girl in love with the guitar man from Memphis. I had been marooned on holiday in the country with my parents and six siblings; a crowded house in a miner's cottage in Castlemaine. It was one of those long, boring, restless summer holidays stuck in the teenage twilight zone between babysitting and boys; an 'Edge of Reality' when all the world conspires against you, when parents just want 'A Little Less Conversation' from their opinionated offspring who know it all.

It was a prehistoric, pre-digital era, so Elvis by satellite was huge. This was bigger even than the man on the moon. But we didn't have TV, and only had electricity. Evenings consisted of squabbling over Scrabble or cheating to buy Mayfair in Monopoly. Excitement was possums scrabbling on the tin roof.

I was doomed to disappointment. Then, a miracle. With only a couple of hours to go, Miss Cowling, who lived over the road, invited me to watch the broadcast on her ancient Astor. One of those lovely lace and lavender ladies, the backbone of church fetes and the CWA, she had, in some mysterious way, found out that I was desperate to see Elvis live. Perhaps that teenage mooning and swooning, with a bit of sulkiness thrown in for good measure, had done the trick because my parents were glad to see the back of me as I raced triumphantly across the road. Miss Cowling, then in her seventies, told me that, at my age, her pin-up boy had been Richard Tauber. But she must have understood my dazed delight as I watched the King, resplendent in bejewelled cape, perform to his adoring fans. I really was in heaven as she plied me with homemade chocolate cake and lemonade which was all the more delectable because I didn't have to share.

After such a night I started exhibiting serious symptoms of lovesickness as I bought fan mags and books and wore out Elvis albums. I even had a tiny crush on a neighbourhood boy because he looked like Elvis in one of the *Kid Galahad* promotional shots. My parents, with their 'Suspicious Minds', worried about Elvis and his pelvis. Those 'Jailhouse Rock' gyrations were not quite the thing for a convent girl from Kew who had grown up listening to the Seekers and Bobby Limb's *Sound of Music*. Overnight Donny Osmond was dumped and I went from good Catholic girl to fanatical Presleyterian.

On the black-and-white TV, I just couldn't take my eyes off him. Where was I meant to look when he shuddered sinuously in my direction? I squirmed with embarrassment as the family sat around the box. With between five and nine of us on the back porch it was pretty cosy *en famille*. My face flamed and my insides tingled, a sort of *Harum Scarum* of untried hormones as his lips latched ... and stayed on whichever bouffant beauty clung tightly to him. That smooching between him and Ann-Margret didn't look like acting to this Ann Marguerite.

My first boyfriend gave me the *Elvis Now* album. A couple of years ago my father ordered from the US a special gospel DVD where Elvis sings hymns that bless my soul. My youngest brother bought me a huge coffee table book covered in white leather with fake blue rhinestones. My other brother has been to his birthplace in Tupelo, was photographed with Lisa Marie in Bendigo recently and has sat in his pink Cadillac wedding car at Graceland. A couple of Christmases ago my husband finally conceded defeat and bought me an eight-DVD pack so I can watch *Blue Hawaii* and *Fun in Acapulco* endlessly, uncritically, forever smitten. Who cares if it's a Hal Wallis B-grader and he's a kissing cousin or a roustabout or a G.I.? These days I can watch and no longer be jealous of all those *Girls! Girls! Girls!* Friends have given me cups and books and pictures and swap cards and other Elvis ephemera. I have an Elvis evening bag and a rotating Elvis light which can transform my small suburban lounge room into the front row at Vegas.

I look at the movies now and marvel at their intoxicating awfulness, the scenes so obviously set in studios when Elvis is surfing, skiing or in a car; clunky backwoods dialogue and bad twisting at the clambake. He is Rick or Chad or Rusty, a kissing cousin or speedway king or scion of an oil tycoon – the roles fairly interchangeable with the usual boy meets girl plot arc and a happy ending on the horizon. I still swoon at his every move as he fronts The Jordanaires or lip-synchs a cheesy love song or clinches any number of rock-a-hula babes in his arms. My husband watches as a silly grin settles on my face and he knows that I'm having a little flurry of fandom and that it's all quite harmless because although Elvis is totally irresistible, he is no actual threat to our marital harmony.

Elvis is 'Always on My Mind'. I still get shivery when he sings 'If I Can Dream'. I love it that 'Little Egypt' is about anything but geography. 'In the Ghetto' is as poignant and true now as it was when he first recorded it in 1967 and 'Return to Sender' always makes me want to sing along. And who hasn't at some time in their lives walked the lonely street of 'Heartbreak Hotel'? Bruce Springsteen was so right when he said that there have been pretenders and contenders but only one King.

I remember how I gave my heart to him as a fifteen-year-old. And somewhere there's still a special spot for him; the spot where grown women smile and remember the wistful ache of that first unrequited passion, when they first whispered dreamily 'Love Me Tender'.

*Music is the mediator between
the spiritual and the sensual life.*

LUDWIG VAN BEETHOVEN

For my eighth birthday, nigh on fifty years ago, I was allowed to invite eight friends to an original screening of *The Sound of Music*. It was so exciting to be taken into town and to huddle into plush seats and gnaw on snowballs as the seven Von Trapp children yodelled through the Austrian Alps. A lifetime later the magic is still there as I watch a school production of sixteen-going-on-seventeen-year-olds put on a great show. Together with those who have lead roles is the dependable chorus; those who people the stage in crowd scenes; those who have a walk-on part or a line or two or a bit of theatrical funny business; those who endow their anonymity with large gestures and visual asides, flamboyant garb or extravagant animation; those who may not have a main role but still want to be noticed; the nuns' chorus at the wedding and all the extras at a Viennese ball where Maria blushes as she dances with the Captain.

I think of the musical director and choreographer who have shaped voices and limbs into near perfect performance readiness. I reminisce about my own effort as Casilda in *The Gondoliers* a generation earlier and know that this is where friendships that last a lifetime are made. I think of the hours and months of rehearsing – the *do-re-mi* of turning up and tuning up and practising again and again till notes are held and dance steps synchronised. I think of cues and butterflies and costume fittings and make-up and the scurrying sounds of stage-hand scene stealers who change the set from convent to chateau. I think of stage fright and parents picking up late, the fledgling romance between the star and the props manager, the bump-out and cast party and the camaraderie created through all the hours of being together; all the thrust and energy that reimagines the original in a school auditorium in Kew.

Reverend Mother reminds Maria, confused by her feelings for the Captain, that she must look for her life. In 'Climb Every Mountain' we, too, are urged to follow every rainbow till we find our dreams. It's a grand anthem about striving to become the best version of ourselves – to look for our own lives, to trust the truth of our feelings, to have something larger than ourselves to hold onto for as long as we live. I am reminded of other popular songs about dreams; Elvis and 'If I Can Dream' and 'The Impossible Dream' from *Man of La Mancha* – 'To be willing to march into Hell for a heavenly cause'. Such songs – rousing secular hymns – make the spirit soar and we recognise that something larger does indeed urge us on.

A season later I watch another school production of *Copacabana*. It's a sassier show with more flounce and flurry and perhaps not quite as earnest as *The Sound of Music*. There's not an empty seat in the house and once the orchestra tunes up all eyes are on the stage. I am amazed at the talent on show. Who could have known that that truculent Year 10 student, behind in her assignment on *Girl With a Pearl Earring*, could dance so brilliantly and execute splits to make us wince and wonder at the same time? And there's that small boy who hasn't started growing yet whose comic timing is something to behold. And another girl who gets lost in the grey zone of the school yard yet can sing and dance like Caroline O'Connor. There are the smiles and high kicks, some good voices and some bad accents and some energetic ensemble scenes. There's a palpable connection between those on stage and those in the seats; the supporting cast of parents and grandparents, friends and siblings and those who just want to see the kids put on a show.

A couple of years ago, I noticed how good one of the dancers in the school production of *Annie* was and wondered what she would do with all that talent. Well, she went to WAPA and is now dancing in *Aladdin* at the Regent Theatre and will become one of the girl group singing starlets in the next incarnation of *Jersey Boys*. More recently, I have watched my daughter in the Gilbert and Sullivan Opera Company's performance of *The Mikado*. She is one of the dependable chorus. However, she still manages her own little sideshow as she acts up, googly-eyed and startled, at the goings-on in the Kingdom of Titipu. She shuffles appropriately in her blue and white kimono and top-knotted, heavily lacquered hair and pretend-talks animatedly to the other lower caste cast members. I laugh at the mayhem and am reminded how compelling and clever the right combination of music and lyrics can be. And a little bit, or a lot, of levity is needed when the world gets too serious. I also wonder if she isn't reliving a bit of my life almost forty years ago when I, too, was in a chorus line, singing well and acting badly, and desperate for the clever line or the cameo or the male lead to notice me. He didn't!

To see an audience rollicking with laughter is a balm for the sore spirit. What wonders can be enjoyed when we are transported by laughter or great scriptwriting or acting that moves us to other places because, somehow, our own lives are on show. What fun we have when the orchestra plunges into the opening number, the auditorium darkens, the curtains open and all the world's a stage.

It's one of my favourite things!

... I loved and guessed at you, you construed me
And loved me for what might or might not be —
Nay, weights and measures do us both a wrong.
For verily love knows not 'mine' or 'thine;'
With separate 'I' and 'thou' free love has done,
For one is both and both are one in love: ...

CHRISTINA ROSSETTI, *I loved you first: but afterwards your love*

It was the biggest house in the street for the biggest family in the street and we O'Neills were it. McKean Street, Box Hill, the middle of middle-class Australia and we were stuck there.

I was especially stuck because I was the oldest of

seven little Australians and my parents needed me to be a little mother to the not-quite-surprise child of later life with his bright red curly hair, small astigmatism and long pale tadpole body. So life consisted of school and homework during the week with the domestic roster of allocated 'little jobs' taped to the kitchen door to be ticked off when completed. Weekends centred around looking after the baby between Saturday netball and Sunday Mass, more homework and then Walt Disney on the back porch *en famille* just before dinner on Sunday night.

So there I was at fourteen, a little bit hormonal, looking furtively at boys on the bus; me, chubby in my grey school uniform and hat and gloves wedged on, and the buck teeth that had not yet been straightened and in charge of a small feral tribe of similarly attired little grey girl slugs. After school, we'd amble down to the bus stop and occasionally I'd treat my entourage to the contents of a small white paper bag of 10 cents worth of mixed lollies or some iced and jammy offcuts from the bakery. Ah, the days of freckles and clinkers and bananas and milk bottles and musk sticks and fragments of neenish tart.

I had had a few crushes before; those of the innocent and unattainable variety which always seem real because they are so impossible. I had broken my father's heart when, at five years old and with absolute conviction, I told him that I loved Ron Barassi, the famed footballer. At twelve, I had pictures of Billy Barrot, the Richmond centreman, taped to my bedhead. At thirteen I had a puppy love infatuation with Donny Osmond, whilst two-timing him with yearning looks at David Cassidy, and later I had a bit of secret adoration for a boy who lived five doors up the street.

And then my universe changed. I'd fallen quiveringly in love with Elvis – and his pelvis – and I would imagine long lingering Hawaiian love scenes and long luscious kisses from the King. I wanted so much to be his rock-a-hula baby. But to tell the truth, my first kiss was a quick peck at six weeks and three days after my seventeenth birthday. I was in my school uniform, all grey and gluggy, hanging around hopefully at a certain Kew tram stop when a tall, clever, spotty boy still growing into himself with his size 11 shoes and witty repartee actually kissed me.

I can still feel my lips tingling almost forty years later.

It was not the Hollywood pash of my cinematic dreams, nor the passionate clinch of secret assignation. It was certainly not the dutiful kiss reserved for spinster aunties or the squelchy mouthworks I'd seen some of the golden older girls engage in with gusto.

It was just two seconds' worth of heaven and suddenly I wasn't a grey little girl slug anymore.

I was a butterfly.

This is an edited version of an article previously published in *The Weekend Australian*, October 2020.

Poetry, the best words in the best order.

SAMUEL TAYLOR COLERIDGE

Poem – a polite four-letter word that is often greeted by a collective groan when mentioned in front of an adolescent audience. It comes with connotations of boring, big words, dead old guys and lots of stressed syllables. It has a reputation for being arcane or obscure, as having nothing of relevance to say. It is outdated, redundant, past its use-by date in a world where language has been depleted into the quick bite for TV and bullet points for the PowerPoint.

But poetry doesn't have to be out of reach or on a rarefied metaphysical plane. It doesn't have to drip with mythological reference and literary allusion. It can be pedestrian, prosaic, mediocre. It can be you or me, jotting down the unguarded thought or the flashing image, distilling in our own vernacular words, feelings and experiences that can be shared with others. Even bad poetry allows us to say how we feel, even if it is clogged up with clichés and undergraduate verbiage and now overpopulates the World Wide Web.

Samuel Taylor Coleridge wrote that poetry was simply 'the best words in the best order'. Poetry is a lyrical linguistic shorthand. The hoary heavy-handedness of prose is dispensed with and a lighter, more revelatory touch is used to prise open understanding and bewitch with wonder. Fortunately, today's students can have fun with poetry. They can create their own poetry by drawing on their own knowledge and experience. While putting words into action, or poetry into motion, they learn about rhyme and rhythm, metre and beat. If recent Nobel Prize in Literature winner Bob Dylan put words to music as the troubadour of the 60s, will Billie Eilish tell of the disaffection of the Gen Z kids? Eilish's 'everything i wanted' is a raw poetic cry in a televisual medium; poetry for the pubescent populace.

With our students, poetry is now off the page and into performance. Rap rules with its street beat and everyday argot. For too long poetry has been a prisoner to the scholarly and academic, to those studying literature or to the truly erudite. But now it's on the run, escaping into the minds and imaginations of children all over the country, leaving ardent acolytes breathless in its wake. Primary students are entranced by *Poems to Make You Puke* where spaghetti rhymes with confetti and snot with grot. They love the rudey bits, festering fertile ground for their own revolting rhymes.

Our first poetry is the poetry of the womb where we learn to recognise speech and silence, the euphony of existence, and where the rhythm of life becomes a powerful beat. Then comes the poetry of the lullaby, the croon and swoon of maternal benediction. Nursery rhymes follow shortly after. Then comes the poetry of the playground; the chants and counting games that change as each year's Preps grow up. A new playground patois updates 'Apple on a stick' for its current incarnation on the asphalt at lunchtime.

As we go through school we learn about great and minor poets, those who never bettered their juvenilia and those whose words still thrill and exalt. I recall learning Alfred Noyes' 'The Highwayman' in the early 1970s where 'the moon was a ghostly galleon tossed upon cloudy seas' and Bess, the landlord's daughter, warned her lover by shooting herself with a musket as over the cobbles he clattered and clanged, 'Riding, riding'. When I meet school friends we reminisce about the poems of our past: John O' Brien's 'Said Hanrahan' with its antiphonal 'We'll all be rooned', Banjo Paterson's 'The Man from Snowy River' and of course, Dorothea Mackellar's 'My Country'. T.S. Eliot always seems to get a look in, too, when we talk about measuring out our lives in coffee spoons. As does Shakespeare with his sonnets and his darling buds of May.

We graduate to the workforce where popular culture cues into the timelessness of the genre. We hear of 'Seasons of mists and mellow fruitfulness' as Daniel Cleaver recites Keats to Bridget Jones. Auden's 'Funeral Blues' is featured in *Four Weddings and a Funeral*. 'He was my North, my South, my East and West' (*The Year's Poetry*, 1938) is a moving elegy from a heart scoured out by the grief and loss of a loved one.

The beauty of poetry is that it can render insight in an inimitable way.

But it can also be obtuse and difficult; recalcitrant. Sometimes it needs to be deciphered, decrypted, in order to create from its silver shards and fragments a meaningful whole. And sometimes it can be misinterpreted, misconstrued, meaning falsely attributed to the pretty confection of words. And we can be tricked by those who are clever enough to put words through hoops and pretend. The Ern Malley saga did just that.

Poetry is the heartbeat of humanity. It can course red and raw in obscene and inflammatory vernacular or it can trickle and tickle in genteel insight. It can make social comment, polemic or satire. It can be furtive or fun or frivolous. It can praise or pillory. Its words can be lovingly shaped into the sweetest soufflé, a taste of heaven compared to the doughy white slice of prose or the soulless language of the public communiqué.

Poetry comes in all sorts of shapes and sizes; alexandrine, villanelle, clerihew and sestina, to name but a few. Doggerel and limerick are beloved of the locker room and the bar. In the tutor groups of academe Paradise is Lost. And romantic Year 10 students discover that Romeo and Juliet are not really a(n) heroic couplet!

Henry Lawson wrote of the backblocks bard who 'takes his pen in tears and triumph' and writes for those who cannot. According to Bernard O'Dowd, a poet's function 'is to chart the day and make it habitable'.

The title of Les Murray's recent anthology, *Learning Human*, aptly sums up what poetry does. It helps us to know who we are. It is the touchstone of universal connection. And, in Melbourne, what of the poetry of football? Bruce Dawe in *Lifecycle* almost apotheosizes those gladiators of the old VFL and his poem is shot through with humour and pathos where 'Carn ... he's a little Tiger!' (*Collected Poems 1954-2005*, 2006) is both a blessing and a curse. Poetry can barrack and shout and exhort. It can lament, lambaste and lampoon. It can enumerate, in Dawe's words, 'the terrible litany of particulars'.

Perhaps Emily Dickinson, the nineteenth century American poet, best distinguishes between prose and poetry:

> They shut me up in Prose –
> As when a little Girl
> They put me in the Closet –
> Because they liked me 'still'

Poetry is anything but still, despite its sometimes reticent demeanour, its fine dressing. It can be a riot of words and images, a kinetic kaleidoscope, compellingly coupled to evoke an emotional response. But for most of us, and for the young poets of our classrooms, one can only agree with the Lebanese poet Kahlil Gibran: 'Poetry is a deal of joy and pain and wonder, with a dash of the dictionary'.

This is an edited version of an article previously published in *The Age*, 27 April 2015.

Hope is a thing with feathers
that perches in the soul.

EMILY DICKINSON

I love the tiny sparrow in its circadian circus flight
Its dips and dives and derring-do from morning,
noon till night
As it stops to briefly gargle and gurgle its good news
On speckled wing and downy prayer to exchange
its worldly views

For a sparrow is a bird that putters in the leaves
And sometime nests suburban-like in the dark of eaves
And keeps a happy, beady eye on the goings-on of folks
Chortling with its feathered friends over the lamest human jokes

A sparrow is no trouble as it flits so fancy free
And hurries home with restless zip to a lemon-scented tree
To chatter loquaciously, up talking with the lark
Non-stop chirpy commentary until after it is dark

God loves the little sparrow in its habit, brown and drear
Congregating faithfully with never-ending cheer
Not worried that the other birds may catch the artist's eye
Happy in its ordinariness, tickling low the sky

With song aburst with joy at adventures way ahead
A serenade for living, a requiem for the dead
God sees this little friendly bird and blesses it in flight
The job complete – it has put my wilting heart to right.

*If you have an eye for it the
world itself is a sacrament.*

SAINT AUGUSTINE

Holidays don't have to be grand tours or beach bliss or discovery adventures. Sometimes they are just a couple of days away from the usual routine; a different bed to sleep on, a momentarily different headspace for the sojourn, some anonymity away from daily recognition and where it locates you in the social landscape. Sometimes holidays are just a quick phone call away, a pleasant train trip to Bendigo and knowing that your brother is glad to see you. At home, the family reconfigures itself in your absence and doesn't miss you too much because you'll be back soon to reinstate a degree of domestic order. So I decide to take a mid-week mini-break up to central Victoria and am happy to spend two hours in unplugged reverie on the train to this goldfields town.

I like Bendigo with its talking trams and wonderful gallery, its country-cousin feel and hotspots of sophistication, its journey to the centre of the earth in the Central Deborah mine, its good pub food, its egalitarianism abroad where popping out to the local shops doesn't involve putting on make-up. And Bendigo has the beautiful Sacred Heart Cathedral. Unlike other great Gothic churches, it is not bathed in an oppressive bluestone gloom where sins shiver just below the skin. Sacred Heart's sandstone spaciousness is alive with light, and the invitation to pray hovers welcomingly in the air.

As I settle into a pew, I am distracted by a sudden swoop above me. Then another. Two little sparrows are playing hide-and-seek in the rafters. They are chortling in sparrow-speak and it's a happy hymn of trills and chirps as they zoom about in this sacred airspace, oblivious to the woman below, or perhaps putting on a performance for a delighted audience of one. I notice a few missing panes of glass through which an adventurous aviator might fly, so I don't worry that they are trapped in some sort of avian Alcatraz. I imagine that during Mass they are duly reverent or are gazed at by cherubic curly-haired toddlers mesmerised by the miracle of flight and the fun and games being played high above them.

I've always liked sparrows – stoic, skittish, plain, hopeful little sentries, rather overlooked when compared to gladiatorial eagles or colourfully clad rosellas or big bad black crows. I like their cheerfulness, their chirrupy conversation, their gossipy greetings as they chat to each other about good food finds in suburban backyards and know where the old lady is who feeds the birds. I like sparrows because they are ordinary feathered friends who have no pretensions about who they are. They accept their place in the bird kingdom and get on with it. They have a welcome sense of community and at night specially chosen trees vibrate with sound as small scufflings take place so each one finds a resting place.

My grandmother loved the sparrows who visited her garden. She would soak her bread crusts so that they would not be too hard to digest and would place a saucer of water out for thirsty visitors. She also had a bird bath where travellers could wash their wings and shake their tail feathers. Their plumage, though the work-a-day brown of an old nun's habit, was primped and plumped up ready for the next big flight. At twilight time, they would swoop in and play amongst the big bosomy hydrangeas and sturdy red geraniums. They were at home amongst the lemon-scented gum trees.

I love these cheerful little choristers. Their song is a full-throated surge of joy, flung melodiously into the air to be caught by those who are alert enough to hear these grace notes all around them. Saint Francis of Assisi surely must have felt the same rapture when he addressed his brother birds as he responded to the hymn and hum of all living things all those centuries ago. Every time I hear the sparrows' chirpy canticle, I am heartened by these chords of creation welcoming another day; another day open to all sorts of flights of happiness and imagination and the knowledge that simply being alive is a blessing.

... those letters are a fairly accurate recollection of the vagabond heart of my younger years ...

My mother kept everything I wrote back home as I sojourned in the United Kingdom in my restless and travelling twenties and thirties. Every blue aerogramme, inked thickly with detail and description, was scrupulously archived along with postcards, printed ephemera and the occasional novella-long letter written in transit between bouts of employment and happy wandering.

Under a kaleidoscopic splash of exclamation marks, dashes, errant apostrophes and bad puns, I can still glimpse the girl I was. In my large open hand, I would dash off commentary as my four sisters and two brothers vicariously hitched a ride with me, their oldest sister, as I criss-crossed the UK and landed the odd jobs that kept body and soul tenuously together.

Dullness of experience or expression was not to be tolerated. In between the spaces, loops and emphatic underlinings of words on the page, small incidents were amplified into larger episodes. Here was a little artistic embellishment, the embroidery required to cover up the banality of long days when only a hot bath and a good book could restore my equanimity. Therewith, a little more adventure sewn into my stories of devil-may-care daffodil picking in Cornwall, clerking and chamber-maiding, singing in a band in the Isle of Man, selling flat-pack kitchens in Wimbledon, ushering in a theatre, running a disco in Guernsey and being in charge of bored city children in a Hampshire holiday camp.

Those letters were written with love, occasional homesickness and an avidity of expression aimed at pretending that long shifts cooking, cleaning and waitressing were really jaunty little escapades with a bit of domestic work thrown in for good measure. So a bit of big, little lying when the weeks were long, but a between-the-lines suggestion that I was right where I wanted to be.

Those letters were lifelines. In them I charted how I felt and where I'd been and trusted that all at home was remaining steadfastly the same. And because I spent hours trying to write well, aware of my father's love for clear expression, my mother's for light amusement, and my siblings' penchant for the dramatic in things unsaid or chronological missteps or episodes not completely rehashed, those letters are a fairly accurate recollection of the vagabond heart of my younger years.

Like my mother, I have kept many of the letters and notes and birthday cards sent to me over the years; from grandparents, siblings, old loves, an exotic aunt, dear friends, people I worked with briefly and had fun with whose names are now receding. We have been connected to each other through blood or circumstance or geography, colouring in each other's lives in significant or incidental ways, being together as only human beings can. I hope I read them again before they become the paper-thin leavings of my life.

I also have all my parents' letters sent between Melbourne and Edinburgh in the late 1950s. I have not read them, bundled as they still are in ribbon, and I wonder if I ever will as it seems like trespassing on the ghosts of lives gone. These are not the lives of the famed or fortunate whose letters are edited or redacted or translated or of important historical or literary consequence. Perhaps they are too close to home to read. Maybe my daughter will read them and with the passage of time she'll get a different glimpse of her grandparents. Perhaps they will be disposed of, unregarded. Dead letters.

To receive a letter when far from home was always a joy. It was something to be savoured, to be read carefully, put away safely, got out again to laugh over, to feel that despite your physical absence you were still right in the middle of things. Family letters were full of who did what and when and what was happening at school and when was I coming home. Friends' letters were full of bad romances and changes of career and advice about travel destinations and when they were coming over. In my eight years away, sometimes it was just seeing familiar handwriting on an envelope that gave me a skip in my step, knowing that as soon as I could, I would rip it open and begin smiling to myself or chortling aloud because the writer knew just what I wanted and needed to know. They knew me.

Perhaps that's what the best letters are – a real communication of understanding and empathy, writing to the person you know and referring to those things that will be of interest; knowing your audience's temperament and disposition and contouring what you say in the most accessible manner. Sometimes there might be encouragement or reassurance or candid advice or some invisible mending in the choice of certain words.

There is an intimacy and uniqueness in a handwritten letter. It has nothing of the mass-produced or pro forma. It celebrates the very human talent for combining affection and information – often with highly individualised efforts at spelling. No wonder letters become keepsakes; they mark our hearts forever, archiving a certain time and place, belonging to that someone else ago who hasn't quite disappeared.

John Donne wrote to Sir Henry Wotton in 1597, 'Sir, more than kisses, letters mingle souls'.

Treasured letters connect us in ways that cannot be measured or analysed or data-derived. They are soul to soul exchanges, intimacies shared, love multiplied, reminders that we matter to others. They are words to make the world go round; their contents mingling souls and transcending time, celebrating what we are to each other.

They are the lines of our lives.

Lifelines.

Life lines.

This is an edited version of an article previously published in *Melbourne Catholic*, 2018.

The years teach much which the days never know.

RALPH WALDO EMERSON

Sometimes you want to visit a place just because the name sings to you. A wrinkle in the otherwise rational, there is some strange cosmic pull that insists that you take the time out and deviate from settled plans to pass through and pay homage. No is not an option. In the single perambulation of a lifetime you may never pass this way again.

This place may be a small black flyspeck between contour lines on a local map. It may be generally unremarkable except to its inhabitants and the few who have accidentally found their way here after taking the wrong turn off a main road. The odd wandering rambler may have trudged into town for reasons to do with the spirit of adventure or out of curiosity or because they know they can get a bed for the night. Perhaps it is part of a day's pleasant detour or a stop on the road less travelled. Or it is legendary in long ago family lore and the ancestral spirit requires obeisance. It may be a place where an improbable notion of romance has been nurtured in the pages of a novel or in the dusky twilight of a half-remembered poem. Perhaps its rustic charms, natural beauty or untainted serenity lure a small returning faithful. Whatever the reason, we sometimes find ourselves in out of the way places that hold their own special delights; places that invite us to the surprise party of discovery in the gentle unspooling of their particular story.

For me, the glorious and irrefutable beckoning of whim is the wind at my back, whooshing me along in its wayfaring, as I seek out such places to satisfy my own map of the world; the unique cartographical, and occasionally capricious, charts that comprise my adventures away from the safe shores of home. And much as I have wandered off the map on my funny little side-tracking jaunts to lesser-known and unheralded spots, it is these places that are being mapped ineffably in my memory; they provide the latitude and longitude of my internal map and compass.

I am found in places that surrender to their surroundings, alert to the rustle and hush, the purr and whisper, the quickening and the glimmer, the sweet lilting exhalation in sourcing joys and trifles on the unscripted journey. They are the thrills and frills of surprised delight, the sudden tableaux, the vignette or cameo; support acts for the traveller who cares to look beyond the obvious; my magpie collection of small shiny wonders and minor elations that furnish a map not yet permanently fixed.

Long ago in the wilderness years/glory days of my middle twenties, I spent two months in late winter picking daffodils in the Cornish countryside near Goonhavern, a couple of miles from the county-seat of Truro. A raggle-taggle backpacking group of antipodeans, all in search of something – or nothing – had fetched up in some basic farmhouse accommodation. Just before the sun tickled the night out of sleep, we were picked up in a truck, driven down bumpy lanes and dropped off in a vast and nodding field. I was identified merely as a number taken randomly from a book of raffle tickets. No name. No pack drill. No tax. No criminal record check or psychometric testing. Nothing personal. We were just a cluster of nomadic seasonal workers, nameless drifters in grubby gumboots marooned in a sea of spritely yellow blooms.

From dawn till dusk we selected strong green stems and sorted them into elastic-banded groups of ten for chic London florists. It was hard work as I stooped and shuffled and snuffled next to a family of Lithuanian

Romanies; seasoned pickers whose crates seemed to fill at an unbelievable speed. My soft spoilt public service hands became red and weepy after a couple of days of pulling sappy stems out of the loam. I plodded glumly through row upon row and only occasionally came close to filling my quota of five crates, each of which contained a hundred bunches. This hardly made the day's work worthwhile from a financial point of view as I handed in my pulpy ticket in exchange for a few pounds.

But the idea of picking daffodils in Cornwall had such a romantic ring that a small amount of suffering was worth the colour that this episode would surely add to my travel stories and tall and sometimes true tales. And if I wanted a day off, no one noticed and no one cared. I was just a number; here today, gone tomorrow, a vanishing spectre or missing person in the strange and precipitate peregrinations of those who seek work in undocumented agricultural employment.

All the while, I wrote long missives to the family. My mother archived everything I sent home: the Isle of Man tourist brochure, the York Minster poster, the recipe for real Dundee cake from Dundee, the pantomime programs from the Wimbledon Theatre, the ferry ticket to Sark and the first Christmas trinkets sent home from Kinloch Rannoch where my later hardened hands withstood the three hour hand-peeling of potatoes for hungry boys' boarding school dinners; the hands that would never have entertained such a job at home. Oh, how travel unravels the insularity and snootiness of the middle class.

Reading those letters now I am transported back to hopeful travels of my earlier years. Without wheels I couldn't get far and I wasn't brave or foolhardy enough to hitchhike along country roads I didn't know, so I regretted not getting much beyond Newquay and its famed waves. An indulgent night in a small bed and breakfast in Penzance was a nod to my flirtation with Gilbert and Sullivan in a 1975 high school musical. I have vague memories of visiting St Ives, but that could have been in another of my lives! St Agnes was just another signposted Cornish village off the beaten track. I liked the name, perhaps something to do with Agnes being the patron saint of Girl Scouts and a nod to my catechism classes where the saints took up righteous residence in malleable young minds. But, alack and alas, I didn't get there in the middle 1980s as other roads beckoned and I looked for, but rarely found, larger adventures.

The next stop then, after all the daffodils were picked and despatched, was chamber-maiding in Dorset at a family-run hotel near Studland. In a blue and white smock clearly identifying my servile status, I lugged linen along corridors, mopped floors, replaced guest soaps and was meant to know my place. When I had a letter about the artist Francis Bacon published in *The Times*, I was summoned to have a small sherry with the minor public school owners of the establishment.

Briefly paraded as a curiosity from the Antipodes, and a bit of an upstart for my temerity in lifting my head above the parapet of purported social station, I was then dismissed back to duties with that particular brand of cold courtesy that aims to keep the classes divided.

In my room in the staff house I would read and write and dream and spend my days off happily pottering around the Isle of Purbeck. The highlight of the week was the Swanage disco where I danced giddily under the glitter ball, slushily happy in the knowledge that this was only a holiday job and that my grown-up life was waiting for me to claim it. Somehow, though, I managed to defer this until well into my middle thirties where I could no longer pretend the magic of such menial jobs was grist to my imaginative mill. Babycham and 'Wake Me Up Before You Go-Go' are my signature memories of this season spent making other people's beds and laying out chocolate truffles on perfectly plumped pillows for Giles and Alice and their SW19 progeny.

After Dorset, there was 'Auntie Annie' at a holiday camp in Hampshire, playing nature games and bingo with bored children who just wanted to go home and doing a guest set with the local beach-boy band on a Saturday night. Then further housekeeping in Guernsey in the Channel Islands, cleaning rooms and spending days off reading or catching the ferry to Jersey, St Malo or Herm for a change of scenery. After that, and with a chronology that is more big-picture than deadly factual and where I seem to have lost a few weeks, there was work as an administrator for a builder in South London and some nights helping out in a nursing home. There was a brief stint at an estate agents and sandwich-making for hungry students at a polytechnic near Putney. Then, three years selling self-assemble furniture by day and ice cream at the Wimbledon Theatre by night. Tucked away in those years are all the other casual little jobs that come with travelling: clerk, barmaid, cook at The Dog and Duck in North Wembley, hostess and singer in a reception band on the Isle of Man, a not very good waitress anywhere. All the while I put off *growing up* with my misplaced faith in the reliability of the heart. In those long-ago days before the instant documentation of every love-gone-wrong moment, there is, I am glad to say, no photographic evidence of anything I would not want my mother to see.

Anything.

Fast forward almost thirty years and I am back in Cornwall and this time I am visiting St Agnes on the rugged northern coastline. I am now married and have a Glaswegian mother-in-law and a daughter at home who resolutely refuses to miss me. In some ways this is a little pilgrimage for me so I can send my mother-in-law a postcard from the village that bears her name. And she is a saint, in her warm no-nonsense practical way, the sort of latter-day domestic saint that so many women are who survived the Blitz in a London underground tunnel. She is a saint of making do and getting on and being grateful for every bit of joy that comes into her life. My daughter adores her.

She loves me almost more than her own son whose reliability of heart tethers me even in my most wanderlusting days. I am happily on my own travelling with the whim beneath my wings. I take a local bus from Truro and am swished through the countryside with its abandoned tin mines and little stone churches, its farmhouses and villages with fairy tale names. On the top deck, a man in a tatty anorak is muttering to himself as he flicks impatiently through maps. A couple of teenagers laugh and lurch towards the back seats for a sneaky smoke. I huddle right above the driver so I can scan the horizon. I don't want to miss a thing – the choreography of clouds as they scuttle overhead or the glimpsed view of a seething sea or the spire of a church in the dim distance. I'm on top of the world as leaves and branches thrash the windows along canopied lanes and B roads. Without seatbelts it's a bit big dipperish in the front seat, with its panoramic view over the sweeps and folds and undulations of the coast, but that's a small price for admission on this away day.

I arrive in St Agnes, via a stop at the beach at Perranporth, and disembark, checking the return times with the driver. It's a drizzly day, with the sea growly and prowly as waves splatter the shore, but I am tea-cosy warm and ready for anything. At the local museum I gaze at lives of hardship, frozen now in history behind glass display cabinets, dated and curated into local lore. The black-and-white photos of long-ago school children, dressed and pressed into neat Victorian rows, intimate the hovering reality of mortality. Miners grin as they emerge from their sooty subterranean burrows. I buy a couple of bookmarks inscribed with the words 'St Agnes' and a gold turtle tooled into the red leather. I sign the visitors' book with a flourish. It's been a good nine months since anyone from Melbourne has been here.

There's always something so real about signing my name. It's a validation of sorts, a way of saying that I passed through, if but once. It's a personal marker, my signature, announcing the blood and bone reality of my existence; me, a scintilla of struggling stardust in the face of the monstrous maw of eternity. I am briefly embodied in time's infinite ledger. Like carving a name into a tree or on a desk or into wet concrete, I want to live beyond the confinements of my mortal tenure. A passer-by may one day stop and wonder, as I often do, at these bespoke entries, these incontrovertible claims to existence of one who lived her destined years on this small planet that spins like a top in an inky infinity. I wonder about the names above mine and the places the writer has come from – Connecticut, Wales, Johannesburg. I read their comments and observations and feel the plaintive tug of the human condition in every entry. I enjoy the careful copperplate of an older hand and a child's concentrated cursive effort to write themselves into their life and times; to own and name exactly who they are.

In my various sojourns I have appreciated the calligraphic flourish of some signatures and mused over the blocky splodges of others. I have marvelled at the vast miscellany of style and the handwritten hieroglyphs of those who seem to hide behind their names. I have been grateful for legibility and an assured hand and have wondered if one can really determine the content of a character through the science of interpretation, graphology. Perhaps my signature might not stand up to such scrutiny. It may say more about me than I care to divulge.

Enjoying an Edinburgh Festival in those years that got away I visited St Peter's Morningside to see my own parents' signatures in the registry book that recorded their marriage in December 1956; a neat ten months before I was born. My mother's signature has carried over into mine with its legibility and clarity and general uprightness. However, I have since developed something of an autographical zest for signing my name and I'm not quite sure what that means or if I'd really want to find out. I treasure my father's diary for the year 1957 where I am written into existence for the first time ever as he records my birth in late October in a clear and certain hand that leans forward expectantly.

Up and down the United Kingdom I have signed guest and visitor books where I comment dutifully on bed and breakfast hospitality and the full English breakfast. But it is the bound and brooding books in churches that entreat a prayer from passers-by that really speak to me. In small bluestone chapels, hundreds of years old and with the story of generations inscribed on plaques and paving stones, I have quietly penned the changing hopes of my vagabond heart.

I have written prayers in Paris and in Bendigo and Balwyn, in cold Rosslyn Chapel, in modest churches and great cathedrals, in cosmopolitan conurbations and secret idylls; the book always open to the spiritual terrain of my various journeys. Nothing too eloquent, just the usual concerns and gratitude and the odd intercession to the saint on duty that day. Writing so I have made my mark. Visible ink makes me live. Sometimes, I have been so enamoured of the other heartfelt human pleas for divine intervention that I have given scant attention to the splendours of stained glass and sculpture. I have heard a heart weep behind faint etchings of sorrow. Sometimes, an impotent anger lay between the lines that scored the page sharply and torment resided in the scrawl that beseeched forgiveness. In firm fonts or spidery hieroglyphs, the hearts of those writing to God were wrenched right open; letters from believers and letters from those who had nothing left to believe, all mining the deep wounds of living in their own hand. Occasionally, there was a swooping script of wonderment and thanks, an almost incredulous utterance because prayers had, somehow, been answered.

In this digital age, I cling fast to the sweep and curl and stroke of the handwritten. Behind the dots and dashes, the artistic and indecipherable, the arabesque and the functional, there is still and always someone saying, 'I was here'.

In St Agnes I dawdle and dally, nosily peeking over fences and into kitchen windows, imagining other lives and other times. I turn into wooded lanes where the mush of leaves lies underfoot and the air is tinged with sweet and sour wood smoke. A sinuous black cat is a good sign. Crusted coves whisper their briny secrets in the froth and foam of the incoming tide. I imagine the smuggling of pirate days and contraband lost to the spume and spittle of angry waves. I take arty photos that feature sea and sky in elemental rhapsody. Really, they're just photos taken at odd angles with an imposed quirkiness that doesn't quite work. I buy a 60p postcard to send to Nana who is now only called Agnes for official purposes. She will be thrilled to receive it.

In the main street, the St Agnes Miners and Mechanics Institute is now a café/community centre and I settle with a cup of tea and a real Cornish pasty to collect my thoughts. I jot down my impressions of this small stone village, quick pen strokes in my own oversized shorthand. I seize the mood and moment, doodling and dashing off words and sprinkling adjectives like hundreds and thousands into a layer-cake of descriptive prose. I worry that purple is the predominant colour and that I am still guilty of the florid. I sit for over an hour, a refugee from the gloaming that has leached the colour out of the early afternoon. At my table for one I read *The Times*, write another few postcards and listen to the music of the local accent. On BBC Radio Matt Monro sings 'Magic Moments'. Bathed in the sudden exultation of being alive, healthy, with time on my side and loved ones waiting for my return, I acknowledge that I am, indeed, a happy wanderer. I have ticked off this small destination; this village with its population of just over a thousand and its own unique history and its lovely name. I have had the joy of satisfying nothing more than a whim. One of these years I will visit St Anne's on the Channel Island of Alderney. I will do this just because it shares my name and because I didn't get around to it when I lived and worked in Guernsey for eighteen months in those tumultuous twenties when my heart was a hunter and my mind was slowly being prised open.

Whim. What a wonderful way to travel. No one is expecting me home at any hour, although I have let the proprietress at the bed and breakfast know what I am doing. I do not have a phone on me. I am free to inhabit the role of bystander, observer, shadow player, extra, that unknown woman in a crowd scene, that lady with the slice of bright pink hair in the queue for the local bus; all perfect little walk-ons. I scribble down notes, thinking about people and history and life and what it all means, a bit of cod philosophy, revelling in my few days alone. I am wrapped up in the luxury of my own untrammelled time. Without the weight of work to get up for, I have a spring in my step and an adventurousness that is kept well-hidden at home.

Then it's the long flight back to my real life as an English teacher in suburban Melbourne, and someone for whom Wordsworth's famous poem *Daffodils* will always have a special resonance. Next time I visit 'the green and sceptr'd isle' I will have my daughter in tow. I'll point out some of the other landmarks of my life, long before I met her father, when I was still learning to be me; when I was someone else.

I will not tell her all my true stories.

I hope that she will travel well and gently, with the occasional beckoning of whim to illuminate her own adventures. I hope that she will glimpse the small and shy and slow and serendipitous away from the express lane of life's busy journey, that dire juggernaut of forward momentum. I hope she will dawdle and daydream as I have done and move off the map occasionally.

I hope that when she comes to the age of comforting reminiscence that she, too, will look back in rose-coloured reverie. The landscape of her heart will include surprises, delights and opportunities taken – and forsaken – as she travelled in the direction that sang to her. She too will have the expurgated versions of her adventures shaped agreeably for family consumption. In the legerdemain of life's lottery, she will reach her destination which may double as her destiny.

Yes, there were times when I was cold and hungry and had to sleep on someone's couch and missed my train connections and relied on the kindness of strangers and couldn't make myself understood. But somehow a bit of nostalgic revisionism has coloured my stories happy.

I wouldn't change a thing.

It is good to be unselfish and generous, but don't carry that too far. It will not do to give yourself to be melted down for the tallow trade; you must know where to find yourself.

GEORGE ELIOT

My favourite writing place thirty years ago was a third-floor harbour-front coffee shop in Creaseys department store located in the main street of St Peter Port, Guernsey. Here I would sit for hours, slowly sipping the cooling clouds in my coffee. In this eyrie, I had a postcard perfect view of the islands of Herm and Sark, and on blessedly clear blue days Alderney would shimmer on the horizon. Occasionally, I would get dark stares from staff for occupying the prime viewing spot. With my notes and pens and papers, I used my day off from strenuous chamber-maiding to write long and adjectivally dense letters home.

I am now on my self-titled *nostalgia* tour – hauling my daughter down long and winding memory lanes as I revisit old haunts. She has happily agreed to be my all-expenses-paid travelling companion, so our arrangements are most congenial. We are to have a week here so I can show her the places where I did the jobs that are not part of the later professional CV; the jobs that come with travelling and the urge to stay or go and the need to keep body and soul together in the interim. So on a lovely day in the middle of the northern summer we sit at a window table in Creaseys for a good two hours as locals meet and greet. The baked potato and coffee will do the trick in not having us feel guilty about hogging the best seats in the house. I hear the gentle patois of chat and cheer. The harbour below is busy with fishermen and day trippers from St Malo and a percussive rattling of masts and sails in the marina ricochets on a gentle swell of wind. I gaze out over 800-year-old Castle Cornet and see small boats jostling and the Condor ferry readying for departure. A giant cruise ship is berthed a long way out and has disgorged a phalanx of rotund Americans in Disney T-shirts who will do the island in six hours.

The next day we take a long walk up Rohais Road

and continue to be amazed at the politeness of the local drivers. Gridlock here is three cars on the roundabout. The hotel I worked at is now just hanging onto three stars, a vast remove from its glory days in the mid-1980s with its new golf course and luxury spa and beauty salon and the in-house staff who thought they were a cut above in their laundered white uniforms and name tags. The chrome brightness everywhere is not retro, just ugly. My daughter and I have lunch in the bistro and we are nice to the nervous French waiter who stutters a bit as he takes our order.

Those of us who have done the waitressing, bar work, cleaning, cooking, laundering, any sort of service work in hospitality or retail know that customers can range from those who treat you as a human being doing a job to those who believe you belong to some form of sub-species. I am always mindful that some people doing these jobs are supporting families and are not just filling in with some holiday shifts between terms at university. They are on their feet much of the day and need to pirouette around the needs and demands of all sorts of paying guests. All work confers a dignity, no matter what it is and at what stage of life you do it, so it is important to see the person in the job, generally doing their best to make your experience a pleasant one. We can choose how we treat those who housekeep in hotels and those who serve us expensive meals as we holiday away from our real lives. I choose to be understanding. I have done my share of domestic drudgery as I have travelled and have an insider's knowledge of just how demanding these jobs can be.

I remember the days of working at the St Pierre Park Hotel and having to clean thirteen rooms before one o'clock, regardless of whether they were left relatively clean or had been trashed by barrow-boy-bankers on long weekend jaunts from London. My uniform was blue and white cotton check and I was little more than a nameless serf. I would trundle a trolley-load of fresh sheets, pillow cases and towels and replenish the shampoo and conditioner and the guest bath soap. I knew just how far under the bed to wield the vacuum and the importance of folding the four-ply toilet paper just so into a neat triangle on its dispenser.

I once turned down David Suchet's counterpane in a family-run hotel in Studland, Dorset. It was one of those rather quaint old-fashioned duties where we would turn down the bedding and place a chocolate on the pillow and adjust the bedside lighting so that daylight dwindled seamlessly into evening. It was like something out of Miss Marple's Bertram's Hotel, with its hierarchy of hospitality and night managers in almost lordly attire checking that the decanters were full and the antimacassars perfectly aligned in the residents' lounge. Perhaps there was even a palm court trio, but maybe I'm letting my imagination run away with me. I never actually saw the great actor who had just started on the *Poirot* series, but corridor rumour was that he was awfully nice. Besides, we chambermaids had a duty to remain invisible and to not intrude on the notice of paying guests. We knew our place, smiled subserviently, and would later eviscerate their assumed airs and graces with much hilarity in the staffroom.

I'm not sure what my daughter has made of her mother's charring and chamber-maiding days. She has been given the broad brushstroke tour, the expurgated version, the rose-coloured revisionism. What she has learnt is that the made bed and emptied bin, the fresh towels and new biscuits with the tea and coffee do not just appear as if by magic. An unsung chambermaid has had to reach her quota of rooms by one o'clock before the next night's guests book in. She has had to spray and wipe, sprinkle and perfume, flush and fix, smooth and plump, empty and refill.

She deserves a tip.

I am no bird; and no net ensnares me:
I am a free human being with an independent will.

CHARLOTTE BRONTË, *Jane Eyre*

Growing up in Melbourne in the 1970s there was an expectation that one day I'd marry, have children and be provided for in an arrangement that seemed more like a compromise than the meeting of hearts and minds of which I had dreamed. At school, we had the *talk* from a doyenne of society about domestic duty and being interested in our husband's career, ready to greet him with enthusiastic delight and a small sherry as he arrived home after a hard day at work. The dutiful homemaker/meek helpmeet model was still in vogue, with priority given to his life and his career and his comfort as we were instructed to sublimate all our desires. However, my friends and I had worked out that this was a load of old washing and that we all had to make our own way in the world. We were all aiming for university, but this was in the days before careers advisors and psychological counselling and aptitude testing, so getting into uni was it – and the rest would fall into place. Still, this did not stop my girlish dreams of Prince Charming swooping me up into connubial bliss. My education may have been middle-class, conservative and religious, but I was no *princess*. There's not much room for being a princess when you are the oldest of seven siblings.

Women of my vintage (a tad older than Virginia Haussegger, a decade younger than Bettina Arndt) straddle the seesaw of feminism. We have adopted or adapted feminist ideas or principles and thrown the ingredients into the blender of modern life. For most, what comes out is a unique confection made up of intangibles, such as personality, background, peer group, domestic situation, employment, ethnicity, socio-economic status and future aspirations – and the history of our treatment by the men in our lives: fathers, brothers, husbands, boyfriends, colleagues and bosses.

There is no cookie-cutter stereotype for any woman who may or may not use this feisty 'f' word. I look at the women I admire, and they are artists and doctors and mothers and religious sisters and my own four siblings. Some are accidental feminists and others are more assertive; each with their own way of being a woman in today's world. They are women whose lives move beyond self to other; women who are funny, fervent and fearless and women who are quietly getting on with things with grit and grace.

I worked hard at school and did the mandatory language, Italian, because I wasn't up to the Maths and I needed one or other of these for university entrance. Those were the days when you could pass (51!) by singing a rather flamboyant Italian version of 'You Don't Have to Say You Love Me' to the assessors as your oral component. It didn't hurt that I received a Special Distinction for English and my name is now languishing on an honour board somewhere in a dark corridor at my *alma mater*. Sometimes, I think I peaked at eighteen and am still trying to capture that rare moment of public adulation. I now tell my students that persistence is one of the qualities that really matters if you ever want to feel you have finally won through.

I have always been a trying woman.

I finished school in 1975, a few years after Helen Reddy's anthem 'I Am Woman' hit the charts and galvanised popular sentiment. Perhaps I was naïve, still bubble-wrapped in relative privilege and myopia. I did not need to roar as many other women did because my choices and chances were right in front of me. At university I had a lot of fun and didn't work as hard as I could or should have. I laughed a lot in the Baillieu

Library and spent time in Café Paradiso in Lygon Street philosophising badly and bibulously over bottles of Mateus Rosé. I did some very un-method amateur acting in Law Revues with a young Steve Vizard and had the odd line or a song in a couple of Tin Alley shows. I had a walk-on in a Feydeau farce and was a short and shiny member of a spandexed K-Tel trio who did approximate doo-wop backing vocals.

Of course, the boys were the directors and stars and chief rabble-rousers, but I made the most of my wonky cameos. I cleaned and babysat to pay the rent on the Hawthorn bedsit I shared with my sister. I played netball for a season and didn't mind a bit of good-natured biffo behind the play. I spent a lot of time in the John Medley building having tea and biscuits for 20 cents and being a twenty-something who had no idea where my future lay, lurching along in a happy sort of mediocrity. The turgidity of my handwritten essays and very poor referencing makes me cringe now. Gillian Triggs was lecturing in law while I was catching up with friends on the lawn outside. It's exactly where my daughter is now – in those in-between years of study and travel and broken hearts and keeping a tally of the kitty in shared houses. And the boys I knew were friends – and still are forty years later.

Into the workforce, the Victorian Public Service, I learned to get on with the job. I never traded on my gender, nor did I ever feel that being female barred me from participation or promotion. Maybe my feminist antennae were not finely tuned enough. Somehow I had not exfoliated myself into a state of thin skin where every action, word or gesture was proof of a hegemonic patriarchy designed to make me feel inferior. Yes, there were extreme cases of braggadocio, the male bluff and bluster of confidence based on an assumed superiority, but by middle management incompetence usually forestalled further ascension up the ranks. Perhaps I was too modest in my ambition and the humility inspired by a convent education was about restraint and collaboration, rather than any sort of personal aggrandisement.

We had been taught to be self-effacing and this may have been interpreted as submissive, which it never really was. We just weren't loud and look-at-me and I am so glad that my daughter will enter a workforce that will be less gendered in favour of mediocre males over conscientious but reticent females. However, there is still a place for humility in a world where every minor accomplishment is lauded with outsize fanfare. Some of the best women (and best men) I know do wonderful things without bragging about it. As with everything to do with our personal interactions in the workplace, at home, with friends, and online, we need to be judicious in when and how we use our particular armoury of attributes. There are times to be silent, as well as times to speak up and out; times to advertise and advocate; times to let others have their moment.

Maybe I wasn't wired with the need to play the boys'

games. Perhaps the having-it-all message meant that I had a choice to do things my way, even if that way was, on occasion, misguided. And in the 1980s when big hair and power dressing seemed to be the thing, I was doing a gypsy boho look, playing my own game, and then throwing it all up to spend eight years in responsibility-free peregrinations abroad. And certainly, my mother was something of a role model; a woman who may not have overtly identified as feminist or read Germaine Greer's *The Female Eunuch*, but one who encouraged us all to follow our dreams; dreams that had all to do with self-worth and self-sufficiency and perhaps a little bit of maverick determination to be different.

For me, practical feminism means equity in action. At home, it means that my husband understands that the value of my time is just as important as the value of his time. I don't have to be a domestic goddess á la Nigella and he can do the laundry. My workplace effort is just as important as his. And with the Rubenesque bloom of my middle years I am much relieved that fat is no longer a feminist issue.

In 1913 the novelist Rebecca West wrote, 'I myself have never been able to find out precisely what feminism is: I only know that people call me a feminist whenever I express sentiments that differentiate me from a doormat, or a prostitute' (*The Young Rebecca: Writings 1911–1917*, 1982). The feminism I want to pass on to my daughter is one that says she can be her own woman and take her place in the world. If she appropriates a version of feminism that works for her and maintains her integrity and sense of justice, I couldn't be happier.

As a woman and mother and teacher in a girls' school, and in a world where social media decides the latest incarnation of the feminine, I hope that young women will have models and mentors that enable them to make good decisions about who and how they are in the world. I pray that they will be engaged in activity that is personally fulfilling and that their participation will enable them to feel and be valued. More than the educational literacy and numeracy they will acquire, I hope they become socially literate. This means being able to read people, to mix comfortably, borderlessly, to be sensitive to the stories of others. I hope their privilege flowers with compassion, that this generation will 'make poverty history'.

For the young woman who is my daughter: I want her to think for herself, to dream and believe. I want her to have favourite songs, special places, a good heart. I want her to hold close those secrets stitched into her soul. I want her to have faith and hope and charity. I want her imagination to take her on incredible journeys. I want her to see the world in all its beauty. I want her life to be painted in bold colour; sunflower yellow and magenta and violet and lapis lazuli.

But for all that, what I want may not be what she wants.

She'll choose her own passions and her own path. And that is as it should be.

I want my daughter and all daughters to be trying women. This means that they keep on, persist, face obstacles with grace and resilience, sometimes tough it out, fail forward, be kind, listen to each other, try when it's hard, speak up, laugh, and give each day their best effort as they build these days into a life worth living.

It means they recognise that womanhood, in all its guises, is a gift.

This is an edited version of an article previously published in *Melbourne Catholic*, March 2019.

This world, after all our science and sciences, is still a miracle; wonderful, inscrutable, magical and more, to whosoever will think of it.

THOMAS CARLYLE

Sometimes it seems as if we have forgotten the magic in our lives; the magic already there if only we took the time to notice it, imagined differently or chanced occasionally on the wild, the wonderful or the whimsical. Instead, we focus on the pragmatic, the profit and loss and the mandated outcome. Our lives are ruled by risk assessment and key performance indicators and a deluge of data. How can we recognise any magic if we are constantly constrained by directives and protocols, by the ticking of politically correct boxes, by the hard and fast, yes and no, black and white of institutionalised behaviour, by the insatiability of digital demands, by the algorithms that keep us seeing what we always see?

The wonderland of the imagination resides in a diaphanous dove grey *maybe*.

And maybe and magic are not so far apart. Maybe, if we allow some downtime for daydreaming, for day trips to delight, and the optimism of trying again, trying for the first time, starting over, the magic will reappear. I'm not talking about illusions or Houdini-esque escapes from humdrum jobs, or the stadium spectacles of mass hypnotism. I'm not talking of sorcery or spells or belonging to some sort of magic circle club or murmuring strange invocations to voodoo gods. I'm talking of the fine art of attitude. It's about looking at the world differently and being ready for the surprises that can tap us on the shoulder when we least expect them. It's about being open to the gift of the unexpected and not being so locked down that we cannot deviate from a course when the right moment beckons. It is about slowing down and noticing the intricate detail in the big picture. It is about being responsive to the marvellous minutiae that decorates the incidental in our lives.

One of my small joys is hearing the birds as they greet the dawn, the warbling notes of welcome and chatter as they fuss and flutter between trees and rooves.

It is a music that makes me thankful. In the morning I always look up to the sky to see what it says about the day to come. Sometimes the colours are so gorgeous that it takes my breath away – fiery pink, indigo blush or apocalyptic gold. Sometimes the dull grey lid of winter suggests I get to my destination quickly before the spit and lash of rain reminds me I am (as all Melburnians well know) ransomed to the weather. Sometimes I am just as happy to sit in the local café, read the newspaper, mentally frame my day and nod to other early bird humans who also like to start their day before the sun rises. I enjoy the lick of chocolate on my milky cappuccino and ease myself into the day and its timetabled certainties and occasional surprises. At night, my feathered friends twitter and tumble as the twilight wraps itself around the suburbs, a cheerful chorus with which to close their day's dalliance.

My friend Gemma jokes that her life is a series of squiggly lines. Not for her the straight line or eventless horizon. She is ready for the joys and jolts that the day might throw at her. She is happy to handle the odd bump in the road because this is the grist of real life; she is open to taking a scenic detour that sees different vistas and possibilities. She is not hamstrung by where others might place her in the world or their preoccupations with status and visibility. She is also old enough not to obsess about FOMO (fear of missing out) because she values the tapestry of experience that colours her day; the warp and weft of opportunity and incident that are stitched together in those irreplaceable hours. Besides, being at everything, always in the loop and constantly connected is no guarantee of happiness. The late Carrie Fisher may have said that 'two of the saddest words in the English language are, "What party?"' (*Postcards from the Edge*, 2002), but the person who has their own measure does not worry about not being on other people's invitation lists.

The straight and narrow is, of course, the way to live a moral life, but there is room for other experiences to be cheerfully circuitous and broad. Tucked inside those squiggly lines are secret rooms of desire and delight, places to go to for replenishment and renewal; places in the heart. Behind these accommodating squiggles one can recompose, sort things out, do a bit of a personal audit or an epic reinvention. Behind the squiggles one can shake the dust off, spark up the spirit, shed the dread and emerge ... ready for anything; ready for the serendipity of things coming together in a charmed confluence that choreographs the day in a completely fresh way.

The confinement of straight lines makes life's journey devoid of the colourful scenery of happenstance, coincidence, synchronicity, intuition, kismet, the chink of light that is new awareness, the possibility of miracles – the cosmic cocktail of chance and hope and stars in our eyes. Squiggly lines say 'yes' to a life less ordinary. To rekindle the magic, we need to be ready for it, receptive, tingling with anticipation, wondering just what the day will open to us; that magic waiting somewhere behind each new morning.

Our brightest blazes of gladness are commonly kindled by unexpected sparks.

SAMUEL JOHNSON

I'm on the 7.11 am train to Flinders Street, clackety clack along the railway track, in a crowded last carriage, positioning myself at the door so I can leap off in a single bound at Canterbury, grab a paper, down a coffee, walk the rest of the way to work to open up my laptop at about 8.10 am to see how my day is shaping up and answer the emails that have colonised in digital demand overnight. As I rejig my backpack, I glance out the window. Between tawdry tags and spray can scribble on a defaced warehouse wall, the words 'Happiness is found in your kindness' catch my eye. Twenty seconds out of Chatham and an anonymous urban philosopher's silver and red daubings have set me thinking. I wonder if anyone else in the carriage has seen it. I look to see if anyone else's face is illuminated ... or puzzled, but the other commuters are engrossed in their mobile devices, reading doorstop novels or with their headphones on listening to one of 10,000 tunes. Down behind the barbed wire, the rusted corrugated iron, the palings like missing teeth, and the abandoned 40-gallon drums of industrial debris, a bit of salvation in the squalid. Not religious propaganda or vilification, not political point scoring, just some humble words about the human condition.

Who is it who has so purposefully painted those words? Are they meant for me? Am I reading too much into them? Have others glanced up, seen them and gone back to Facebook hardly bothering to register the strange beauty, the unexpectedness of a gentle thought in the savage ugliness of the urban underbelly? It reminds me of Arthur Stace and his beautiful copperplate *Eternity*, the one-word sermon he wrote half a million times on Sydney's pavements. I wonder if there are other words on other walls by this unknown thinker. I wonder what else he might have to say. And where. A few years ago on a Glen Iris fence in bright yellow were the words, 'It's a beautiful day'. And all that day and for weeks afterwards it was a beautiful day every day and I was glad that some nocturnal eccentric had reminded me of this. And whenever I used to see 'Such is Life' in dribbling daubs on the brick wall outside St Brigid's Primary School on Alexandra Parade I thought of dead Ned and his reputedly last philosophical exhalation as he faced the gallows. It has since been painted away.

I wonder if there is a secret army of thoughtful revolutionaries whose aim is to make the complacent commuter think. Perhaps they go out under cover of night with their ladders and cans to redecorate the wailing walls of suburban dysfunction. Much graffiti is the unedited expression of the disenfranchised. This visual vandalism is their voice, their tag, their identity. It is their existential cry; their *I was here*. They are just one step ahead of the rapid removal team that will obliterate their brief infamy by repainting walls in council approved colours. Perhaps they are raging against the constraints of an alien aesthetic, the us and them of some mythic demographic divide. Perhaps they are, quite graphically, snubbing their noses at those safely sanitised suburbs into which, they don't, and don't want to, fit. Warehouse walls and underpasses, abandoned buildings and hoardings offer a blank canvas on which to express the inexpressible, in words and images writ large.

Normally I abhor graffiti. I dislike its ugly ferocity, its pointlessness, its illiterate grunt, the scabrous scratchings of visual pollution. But sometimes, just sometimes, there is a glistening shard of truth – and it should not be painted over. Those words have been there for well over six months now and each day as I flash by, I check to see that some other aerosol 'artist' hasn't decided to reclaim those bricks in the wall for his own more narcissistic purposes. I'm afraid that one morning it won't be there to put a thoughtful spin on my day, a foundling talisman to remind me to be kind.

I'm scared its brief life will have been snuffed out by a spray can, its few hopeful words lost under the next layer of tormented text. Maybe it's just someone leaving their mark, knowing their little bit of revelation is only temporary. Maybe there's some code between crews that says this has to be left alone. Perhaps there is a recognition that this touches something finer, that it means more than the fat fonts and hieroglyphics of youthful rebels who need to voice their dissatisfactions with both anger and anguish.

This is the anonymous philosopher's billboard. It is his art/heart space with a message for all to see. A gallery open to the travelling public. Admission free.

And if this bit of unexpected truth is painted over, its words lost to another layer of colour and invention, so be it. It has had its shining moment. It has cheered me on the way to work and shaped the start of my working day. It has given me pause for thought. And so, I keep my eyes open, look about me, ever alert for some unexpected epiphany in the bright daubings that paint the wailing walls of our suburbs.

Truths kindle light for truths.

LUCRETIUS

He was working near my desk, installing phones, checking connections, moving furniture. A brawny young man with a shaved head, some exotic tattoos on his rippling muscles and a lovely smile. We passed a few words about the nature of work and then I asked him, 'What do you pack to pursue a dream and what do you leave behind?' This is hardly the usual question to ask a stranger, I'll admit, but we'd been bantering in a friendly way and he had noticed the poster on my filing cabinet. Without skipping a beat, he replied, 'I'd pack my heart'.

This incident reminded me of our childhood

handyman Mr L, a fitter and turner during the week, but a man who spent a good portion of most Saturdays with us, doing lots of odd jobs to do with spouting and taps and wiring and wriggling around under the house. We all owe our lifetime allegiance to the Tigers because he'd listen to the radio and provide a ripe running commentary as to how the Barrott, Clay and Bourke centreline was faring. We admired him for his practical manly skills whilst we all stepped silently around my dear bookish father. It was Mr L who taught my brother to kick the footy. It was Mr L who was in the real world. It was Mr L who somehow enjoyed doing all those tinkering jobs for a family who were all over the place with their passions and enthusiasms; one child horse riding, another at netball, another reading, one just a toddler, two squabbling about clothes and one unaccounted for, probably next door. It was Mr L who knew all our names, had a joke and a bit of a chat to each of us and we responded in kind.

The best words are simple and direct and appreciable to the hearer. They are packed with meaning and intention and avoid big-noting and obfuscation. They are not the weasel words of spin, or vitriol, or superiority, but words with a universal truth at their core. They do not inflame or incite. They are not false or fraudulent or the contrived confections of those who would mislead or take advantage of us. They are not some legalistic fine print full of get-out clauses and disclaimers and strange asterisked verbiage that leaves us stupefied. The best words are direct, purposeful and do not carry any unnecessary baggage. They whisper to the angels of our better selves.

I'm now listening for new voices. They are not the anointed public voices, but the private voices of good men and women who have something worth saying, some gentle and unwavering truth in a world diseased by dissembling; words that hit home. In a post-truth world of fake news, I am listening to clear and eloquent voices that care for more than themselves; not the voices of the sententious or self-serving, but the voices of hope and good counsel who look to the future beyond our own generation. And inside all the good words that buoy me is the reminder to pack my heart wherever I go.

It was an incidental gem in a day's work; an unexpectedly graced moment, reflecting the kaleidoscopic intersections of life all around us. A small shiny shard that somehow let the light in.

*I am the master of my fate,
I am the captain of my soul.*

WILLIAM ERNEST HENLEY

I love the way travel frees you up. You are divested of the trappings of your day-to-day life – the nine-to-five routine, the evening meals, the folding of washing, the meetings where AOB becomes torture as you mentally replay the day and wish you were anywhere else in the world. And then after a year's planning with travel brochures and email confirmations and long service leave cobbled together with annual holidays you finally get back to London. This is the London where you spent the wilderness years of your twenties. In

Wimbledon and Wembley, you sold designer kitchens, charred and chamber-maided, cooked and sang, did the odd jobs that only travel opens up and being away from home invites. This is the London where you grew up enough to return home.

Samuel Johnson reminded his readers in the eighteenth century that if a man was tired of London, he was tired of life. And who could ever be tired of this great heaving historic city? I am pulled again into the spell that this metropolis casts, enchanted and beguiled and wanting to see as much as I can, rummaging through its offerings excitedly, wondering what new discovery will charm me as I sidle through ancient doorways and clamber into big red buses and finally see the Gherkin close-up. I reacquaint myself with the Underground and its tiled and cavernous corridors and enjoy my anonymity and the freedom to visit galleries, to linger at coffee shops and watch the passing promenade, to have no-one expect me home at a certain hour, to read late into the night.

I'm happy to be on my own, a week's grace spent wandering down unexpected alleys and bumping into history at every turn. I find myself at Covent Garden, thrashingly alive with trade and tourism. I seek refuge in St Paul's, the local parish church built by Inigo Jones in 1662. On its internal walls are hung numerous plaques commemorating those whose working lives unfolded on the stage – thespians of great stature and minor roles, of fame and infamy, of soliloquy and song. As I wander along the aisles I am instantly reminded of the great movies and musicals of yesteryear and the stars who shone in them. Apart from the grand marble plaques to luminaries such as Vivien Leigh and Charlie Chaplin there are small brass nameplates noting those whose careers were less visible; the marvellous character actor, the reliable chorus member, the old stager, the comic turn, the va-voom starlet who shone briefly. I notice the plaque dedicated to Alan Jay Lerner which is inscribed 'one brief shining moment', from *Camelot*. I am reminded of the beautiful song, 'If Ever I Should Leave You' and remember the joys of maidenhood when I had a brief movie star crush on Franco Nero who played Lancelot. And, of course, that leads me straight back to Covent Garden and Eliza Doolittle dropping her aitches and selling her small posies as her feckless father Alfred P finally gets to the church on time.

There's a plaque for one Tony Sympson, 'an inspired player of small parts'. I pause to think of all those who play such small parts, all contributing in an inimitable and inestimable way to the whole ensemble. I think Tony Sympson would have been proud of this epitaph.

Small can be inspiring, too.

I've always preferred the wonderful cameo, the great line uttered by a minor character, the unexpected song that steals the show, the small part that shines and is quietly noticed while the main action briefly absorbs and is later forgotten. I have a soft spot for all those who get the honourable mentions, the runners-up, those who may never be the star turn or hear that rapturous applause; those who do their bit to keep the show, life's crazy, un-choreographed, tumultuous season of grace and surprise and joy and heartache, on the road.

Us.

With the bustle outside but a small, sweet hum, I give thanks for our exits and entrances, the small and occasionally inspired roles we are all given to play in the unexpected script of our lives. And I look forward to my many small walk-ons still to come before that final curtain closes and the stage goes dark.

Oh, to be in England
Now that April's there.

ROBERT BROWNING

One of my favourite things to do, on those days that are not driven by visits to great houses and galleries, is to sit on the top deck of a local bus. The vehicle trundles gently down hedge-rowed or stonewalled lanes and sidles through small sleepy villages whose names float from fairy tales. Sometimes the pace almost slows to a stop behind beetling hire cars or on narrow lanes where cows *moo*-ch across the road, ruminating gently. They are in no hurry, least of all when a queue of cars simmers impatiently in both directions. Occasionally, under flashing canopies of sunlit green, there is a frantic skedaddle down deep dips and dales and sensitive older tummies lurch queasily.

One does not generally think of the sedate retired British middle-class as being particularly competitive, except perhaps when it comes to gardening. But that front seat upstairs above the driver with a panoramic view is prized real estate. As the time for departure from the depot nears, there is a determined shuffling in the waiting line, a jostling for pole position. There is a small stretching of aged legs in readiness to dart upstairs and claim the best seats on the bus. Such sojourners come prepared for these long and winding trips with bottles of water and lunch and often a partner who dares not complain. Many are just there for the ride, pleased to be able to see the countryside from a different angle and in relative comfort from their mobile viewing platform. Some know exactly the second, minute and hour that the bus will stop at the market cross or the Red Lion pub or outside the parish church. Some greet the driver with the local burr and exchange pleasantries as they catch the bus into town for shopping. From my vantage point, the land is a patchwork quilt spread out verdantly upon a gentle undulation of hills and downs that fall into the English Channel. A placid sky with a small furrow of cloud only adds to the charm of this moving picture.

I love the small delights of seeing weather vanes, and

cats in windows, and secret gardens and views beyond the trees and steeples in the distance. I love the fact that someone else is driving and the only thing I have to do is to keep my eyes peeled. My daughter/Sherpa/paid companion and I get to Poole early to make sure we are at the front of the queue for the Jurassic Coast Explorer. She is afraid I will do the embarrassing Mum thing and tries to organise me into silence. She is happy to sit downstairs as I claim the upstairs front window seat and fervently hope I do not have to share it with a garrulous local. My luck holds and I settle comfortably into position ready to let the landscape work its magic on me.

A couple of miles out of Weymouth I see a prancing white horse and rider chalked into the hillside above the village of Osmington. This is King George III and it was carved in 1808 and refreshed in 2012 for the London Olympics so that sailing events broadcast from Weymouth could use this arresting natural backdrop. This is a top deck view only; those on the lower level have no idea of the topographical delights engraved into the Dorset hinterland. From the top deck I can see the long sweep of Chesil Beach and the fourteenth century barrel vaulted chapel of St Catherine on top of the hill outside Abbotsbury, a village famed for its swannery, and a scene that could have come straight out of Hardy's Wessex novels. The bus wends its way gently through the lovely village of Burton

Bradstock – postcard-pretty with its thatched roofs and tea-rooms and self-sufficient compactness.

I delight in the names of these quaint little hamlets and larger towns as I take these more leisurely peregrinations across the southern counties. Who wouldn't want to live in the village of Newton Poppleford or Temple Cloud or (murder-less) Midsomer Norton where Roald Dahl spent some of his childhood? Evocative names flash by on my bus days; Charlton All Saints, Matrimony Farm, Kingston Matravers, Sixpenny Handley. I am disappointed when we pass Downton which has no abbey, just a large storage centre with the bus stopping outside the garage on the main street. My heart lifts when I spy the spire of Salisbury Cathedral in the distance.

As the day mellows into evening, I see the sun striking the hills in a moment of crimson incandescence. Unlike many, I am not looking down into a phone as I am National Express-ed on a freeway to my next destination. I am not missing local landmarks that bestrew the countryside with charm. I am looking up, over and beyond to the horizon. Happy on the top deck of a bus, on the road less travelled, I bask in the simple joys of the slow coach.

This is an edited version of an article previously published in *The Weekend Australian*, 2016.

A thing of beauty is a joy forever.

JOHN KEATS

The incidental and hidden treasures of travel are often excavated serendipitously in the great cities of the world. Often these pleasures are not on public view. They are just off the beaten track, on the periphery of popular interest, cordoned-off, in private collections or behind closed doors. Travel, as distinct from tourism, is never about the certainty of destination, but about the delights and challenges of the journey *en passant*; the picture discovered or the object found or a certain enchanting view of water at dusk where the indigo swatch of sky greets the lilac sigh of day's diminuendo.

Travel creates small bugs of obsession; the need to find out, to solve a problem, to go back and check on something tantalisingly and briefly sighted. The traveller, once home, is transformed into an art historian, an amateur detective and a rabid late-night Googler when a mystery beckons. And so back to the Opera Garnier in Paris, to chase not a phantom, but the provenance of a painting spied in a dark corridor, hung high, out of sight even of most of those who wander off to do a bit of exploring on their own. Hidden in the cavernous gloom is a portrait of a ballerina in splendid costume. Perhaps it is her swirling garment of peacock feathers that first catches my eye, or the extravagant headwear or the luscious background. There is something striking about the equilibrium of her pose – her hands outstretched gracefully mid-pirouette. I take a couple of photos on my snap-happy camera, but I am not a good shot. Later, I discover I have amputated the ends of her delicately poised hands.

Over time I ferret out bits of information and learn about the Ballets Russes and the Belle Époque. Just when I think I will never know the subject of this unheralded portrait I stumble across what I need to put a name in the frame. It is the prima ballerina Tamara Karsavina in the role she created in Stravinsky's *Firebird* in 1910.

And then I start researching the artist, Jacques-Émile Blanche, and find out that he moved in rarefied circles and painted many of those whose names are so familiar to us: Marcel Proust, James Joyce, Edgar Degas, Auguste Rodin, Colette, Claude Debussy, Thomas Hardy, John Singer Sargent, to name more than a few. He was what some would dismissively call a society portraitist, a dilettante, moving comfortably in a gilded milieu, the artist for whom everyone who counted wanted to sit. More research and I find that the painting has had a recent triumphant pairing with one by Blanche of Nijinsky who partnered Karsavina in this role; a role that Anna Pavlova refused because she thought Stravinsky's music too *avant-garde*. The firebird has been taken down from her cheerless corridor and cleaned up to dazzle an audience again – this time at an exhibition of the long-neglected Blanche's work at the Fondation Pierre Bergé – Yves Saint Laurent. I also find an Australian connection. Blanche painted Charles Conder and the young Percy Grainger whose portrait is housed at the University of Melbourne.

I love the sumptuousness of the Opera Garnier with its over-the-top opulence, its excess, its theatricality, its centre-stage personality. I love its red and gold private boxes with their whiff of history; ancient encores lingering like a fading melody in the auditorium. I love Chagall's ceiling. I imagine Degas in his regular Monday night seat, planning his rendezvous at the rehearsals of the *corps de ballet* where he will capture the flutter and flounce of tutus. And I see Karsavina, furled in feathers, dazzle and captivate and shock her elegant first night audience in this great Baroque building that crowns the ninth arrondissement.

She must have winked at me as I wandered off to do my own thing at the Opera Garnier all those years ago. My *l'oiseau de feu* has led me on a wonderful dance, a magical mystery tour of discovery and delight.

This is an edited version of an article previously published in *The Weekend Australian*, February 2016.

In between there are Doors.

WILLIAM BLAKE

A threshold is not simply a boundary. It is something that births new creation and energy and identity. It is a dividing line that distinguishes between two different territories, atmospheres and times. It is space where waiting happens, a liminal travellator which moves one from *Before* to *After*. It is a time where nothing much may appear to happen and activity is withheld, suspended, denied, except that things are still going on, imperceptibly and inexorably, in a deep tectonic way that changes us elementally.

It is the story of spring hidden in the depths of winter. It is the *during* of growing change and departure from the previous way of being that becomes the *enduring* of the new life choice. It may be a period of inertia or discontinuity where old certainties have been cast off and new certainties are yet to be wakened. As we navigate a world whose only constant is change, we ready ourselves for the dismantling of old paradigms and the invention of new ones. Sometimes these disruptions are disconcerting as we adapt to new cultural understanding and social expectations. Sometimes there is the mobilisation of effort because of institutional intransigence and the need to open the doors and let new ideas in to recreate how we will live with more compassion, equality and inclusion. Within these periods there are buds of hope opening, buds that will bloom into global betterment, buds that augur a new flourishing.

Liminal moments occur during rites of passage. We move from the expectant woman to mother, from student to graduate as we await university results, from parent to grandparent, from worker to retiree, from child to adolescent to adult. Life events such as the loss of a loved one, divorce or being made redundant can propel us into the liminal state where we are not who we were before. We are in a state of in-betweenness where there is no going back, only a forward momentum that we may or may not recognise at the time. It is no longer life as we have known it. Transformation is taking place, just as it does, immutably, during the seasons of the year. Sometimes, too, this waiting time is simply a holding pattern as the next stage comes to fruition.

Sometimes we do not actually know that we did something for the last time. We look back and know that we will never do it again. It has been consigned to the past. Perhaps we have simply slipped away into a new way of thinking or being without the explosiveness of a Damascene moment. We are entering a new authenticity that energises who we are in the world.

This may mean the letting go of plans and lifestyles and the imposed external limitations that have bound us to one way of being. We can now encounter a path that allows us to thrive in a new fulfillment. Sometimes our old patterns and predilections need to be disrupted so we can claim our better selves.

Liminal moments are portals to the other side of self. They create deep immersive opportunities to touch the sacred. Sometimes these liminal moments are the bliss of sudden consciousness, a sliver of revelation, a lifting up of the soul beyond the confines of the mere here and now, a blaze of cosmic synchronicity, God.

For some, meditation encourages a new spiritual shape as the old self is surrendered. For others, prayer is a portal. You are not the same person after you have prayed as you were before. In that deep concentration of thought and Godly intention, time loses its urgency. It cannot be pinned down, quantified, limited, calibrated into tiny use-by parcels of human immediacy.

It is time written in stardust and the embroidery of the infinite.

Prayer is the original time out!

For me, dawn and dusk have liminal qualities as they act as portals to morning and evening. They are the talismanic in-between. Their very indistinctness is invitational because it is subtle and incremental, those immeasurable moments of moving from darkness into light and vice versa. This is my prayer time. I love the marbled blush of morning when the world is still asleep and hope brims on the horizon; when those otherworldly doors are open and the secret of it all is almost touchable. Before I know it, the clouds have rearranged themselves into apocalyptic gold and within minutes the full promise of morning is heralded. I love the shades of violet that steal in after the sun has set, deep-set tendrils wrapping up the sky in this crepuscular interlude. It is a melancholy time; that wistful evensong, a time for solace and soothing as the day slips away and we wonder if we have used it well. In these liminal moments that bookend my days, I can imagine anything. These moments are mind-altering in their lucidity. They create a new spaciousness within me.

I am on a threshold. The door is open. I can step beyond.

What comes next is meant to be as the day unfolds as it should.

When we find ourselves released from these liminal

times, we step onto the holy ground of the new and recreated. We are moving away and going ahead. We are readying ourselves for the next chapter in life's precious mission possible.

This is an edited version of an article previously published in *Australian Catholics*, Summer 2021.

*Oft when the white, still dawn lifted the skies
and pushed the hills apart, I have felt it
like a glory in my heart.*

EDWIN MARKHAM

Dawn – and the cast of the world's oldest moving picture show assembles for another day's performance.

Mad hatters and ghostly galleons and Old Testament pillars and playdough rabbits and dragons jostle behind the moth-eaten curtain of night.

The cherub-in-charge of clouds barks orders and loudly consults with the cherub-in-charge of climate. Together they decide the order of performance because they know that if they don't start promptly the azure blue sky, hovering hopefully in the wings, will simply stride in and take over. The company of clouds, waiting just beyond the horizon, will be left with bit parts and walk-ons, brief appearances in a cloudy chorus-line, extras in this one-day-only, one-day-ever, production.

Puff pastry clouds will get a chance to star later in the day. They queue behind morose grey clouds that have become mutinous. Black clouds, like the haunted hounds of heaven, mutter rebelliously as chords of thunder are struck. Cotton candy clouds high kick flirtatiously, hoping to catch the eye of the cherub-in-charge of choreography.

Clouds of different shapes and sizes swagger and swirl and scud and skip, impatient to star in their own heavenly half-hour.

Dawn – another opening, another show.

*But let justice roll on like a river,
righteousness like a never-failing stream!*

AMOS 5:24

I believe in the holiness of water. It is the giver of life and the baptismal drenching of initiation and welcome. It is the salty sweat of the brow and the warm wading pool of the womb. It is the vast oceans and small ponds, the rivers and trickles and tributaries that feed the earth. It is the shimmering swathe of soft summer rain and the dancing arabesque jettisoned from old fountains. It is the municipal lake and the foaming crushing rapids of Niagara Falls. It is the slaking of thirst and the cleansing of body. It is deluge after drought, water into wine, tears of joy. It is the spring of hope.

Almost fifteen years ago I visited Lourdes, a small town in the south of France where, in 1858, a young Bernadette Soubirous experienced eighteen apparitions of the Virgin Mary. After these visitations there appeared a spring at the spot in the grotto where the Virgin had appeared; its gushing a miraculous response to a young girl's faith. It became a place to come for healing, a place of pilgrimage for the faithful, the curious, the desperate ... and for those who had no faith left.

The Catholic faith in which I have happily grown old has been coloured by the stories of saints. Bloody martyrdom and grisly endings competed with mystical manifestations and visitations to fuel the imagination and wonder of this Catholic kid. At school we had a grotto and almost every day of my primary and secondary education I walked past the recreated tableau of this famed Marian apparition. Now, back at said school, I still stop occasionally for a quick prayer, remembering the class of 1931, members, perhaps, of the Children of Mary, whose piety and philanthropy built the grotto. A plain new Bernadette has replaced the one of my school days as the original concrete model was abducted sometime in the early 2000s as a prank (getting that back would be a miracle!). I listen to the gentle bubble and burble of recycled water in the recess of the ivy-wreathed cavern, a sound that is calming in the busyness of the school day. And so Bernadette's story took hold of me at a young age and for years has nestled somewhere between magic and miracle.

I promised to bring back some Lourdes water for my mother. Perhaps it was her way of keeping the faith or journeying with me – my mother who was so often in conversation with either Saint Gerard Majella or Saint Jude. There is something reassuring in the cards and crosses and medals, even the garish fridge magnet. They are not simply mementoes of time and place, but small collectables that furnish the faith. They may well be Catholic kitsch, but I love it that dear Papa Francesco beams at me every time I open the freezer.

My own holy water is at the back of a kitchen cupboard in a plastic bottle. I haven't the heart to throw it out because it holds my memory of that joyful pilgrimage. It is a homely reminder that I am a tiny part of the great flowing river of time and tradition, of continuity and disruption, of looking towards eternity, that is the mysterious and magisterial, flawed and often failing, but enduring Catholic continuum.

At night I joined the procession, a hobbling, bobbing, wrinkled ribbon of movement following the illuminated statue of Our Lady held aloft in a glass case. Candles in paper lanterns flickered in the human traffic of the able bodied and the infirm, the fit and the feeble. Hymns were sung in a multitude of languages and the 'Ave Maria' rang out clear into the deep purple night under the Pyrenees.

As I walked, I started to weep. My tears mixed with the gentle evening drizzle and I was moved by this crush of hopeful humanity. I realised that I was participating in something beautiful, something beyond words, something that joins me with the thousands of others who were gathered in her name. I cried because I saw a tough tattooed Liverpudlian with a green mohawk, tartan skirt and bovver boots cheerfully pushing his sick friend in a wheelchair, keeping his spirits up. I cried because I saw love in action. I cried because I saw faith aflame in the kindness of the able-bodied volunteers who carried the sick with a smile and knew that this service was God's best work. I cried because I was one amongst many who, for whatever reason, sang and walked and prayed.

As the pilgrims opened their hearts and the crippled came to be cured, I saw a wonderful thing. I witnessed that most human and holy and enduring of miracles – hope.

This is an edited version of an article previously published in *Melbourne Catholic*, July 2018.

As the family goes, so goes the nation and so goes the whole world in which we live.

SAINT JOHN PAUL II

Mary, the mother of Jesus of Nazareth, is revered as Mother of the Church. Her love for this child shines through two thousand years of history, a love that survived great chasms of despair and touched heaven in its utter selflessness. As the mortal mother of this cherished child, she would have known the vast joys of love for her son. She would have sung him to sleep, cuddled him, kissed him better as he tumbled in toddlerhood, sought to understand him as her own flesh and blood. She would have told him stories and laughed as he grew up and played in the mud and watched the sparrows and wondered, as all mothers do, what would become of her precious son.

She was a refugee as she fled with her small family to Egypt to escape Herod's slaughter of male children.

She looked for Jesus in the Temple as he amazed and mystified the rabbis with his knowledge of the Scriptures.

She was there at the wedding feast of Cana where her son, in an example of divine hospitality, changed water into wine.

She was there at the foot of the cross as her son died. She held his broken body to her breast, her sorrow immortalised in Michelangelo's *La Pieta*.

Over the centuries her image has been the inspiration for artists. She is clothed in blue raiment, her face in serene repose, her demeanour one of grace and gratitude. She is Murillo's Madonna ascending on a fleecy cloud to her celestial home. She is also a hard-working, poor, devout Jewish woman whose skin would have been exfoliated by desert sand, whose hands would have sewn garments and sown crops and kneaded and gleaned and threshed. At her knee, the young Jesus would have learned about his faith, woven as it was into the very fabric of his existence. He would have become accustomed to the prayers and stories and rituals of the Chosen People, their oppression and Exile and their covenantal relationship with God.

My mother taught me the prayers and stories and

rituals of my people. I learned grace before meals, the stories of the saints and whispered my small sins at confession. There was great celebration as I made my first Holy Communion and I still have the black-and-white photo of that day at the Genazzano chapel – me a buck-toothed, freckled, cheerful child of God, perkily pious in my white dress and veil. Over half a century later, I am still that girl – faded freckles and orthodontic work notwithstanding. I was happy in my faith then and I am happy in my faith now. For my mother, Saint Jude was the pin-up saint, the hope of the hopeless, and Saint Anthony was regularly called on to find lost things. We would tag behind her to the Redemptorist Monastery in Kew as she prayed fervently and we, four, five or six of us, prayed distractedly, desperate to get outside and play chasey. She was the one who supervised those mandatory attendances at confession, a job lot of squabbling young sinners who may have fibbed or pinched a sibling or had mean thoughts about a teacher, a small swag of suburban venalities.

My grandmother taught me the mysteries of the rosary and gave me tuppence to light candles in the Ladye Chapel at St Francis' in the city. Those stubby little candles represented my messy efforts at prayer; a bit of wheedling, some thanks and praise, an attempt at deal-making about homework and a pious Amen. When I stayed overnight, we would always recite the rosary; the perfect enunciation of the first few Hail

Marys gradually slipping away from the 'blessed are thee amongst women' to what Malachy McCourt notes as 'a monk swimming'. In the second bedroom I'd settle under a giant eiderdown quilt with a picture of the Sacred Heart above my head. My grandmother would come in to kiss me goodnight and we'd go through the 'God Bless' litany and list. Sometimes my order of petition would change depending on sibling stoushes, but hers invariably stayed the same.

The iconography of devotion decorated her home – crucifixes, a statue of the Infant of Prague, scapulars, medals, holy pictures and other saintly ephemera. Sunday best was for Mass, where she'd meet her bridge and bowling friends. She'd don an armoury of marcasite, a dab of Apple Blossom and her Queen Mother hat and I'd trail happily behind her up the aisle to secure a pew close to the altar. She made frequent novenas and dutifully saved stamps for the missions and put her widow's mite on the collection plate.

We speak often of our fathers in faith. But in the home, it is the mother who makes sure prayers are said. It is the mother whose active example hands on the faith. For children, a mother's actions and devotions, her daily attitude to God in her life, are discernible before they can fully comprehend their own religious heritage, before they can grasp God for themselves.

In Mary's prayer of praise in Luke's gospel, the Magnificat, she rejoices that all generations will call her blessed. We bless all mothers, and grandmothers, and all who keep the faith and pass it on, with love, to the next generation.

Understanding is the reward of faith.
Therefore seek not to understand that thou may believe,
but believe that thou may understand.

SAINT AUGUSTINE

A couple of hours before my mother died, we shared one of the most blessed moments of my life. We took the Eucharist together, just the two of us at her bedside. Father Bob, the priest on call at Box Hill Hospital, came when called and it was his quick response that made all the difference to my lasting memories of my mother's final hours. It was one of the most beautiful mother and daughter sharings we ever had, and I will never forget the joy and tears of it. My mother was ready for the Lord and all her loved ones waiting for her on the other side.

My mother was a cradle-to-grave Catholic. She would cheerfully admit there were times when she was not talking to God. As with most of us, these were times when life seemed to be unravelling, times when she felt God was not paying her any attention. And then there were the other times of novenas and prayers to Saint Gerard Majella and visits to monasteries as part of a fruitful faith life. We children were often part of these suburban pilgrimages to different churches and chapels and got to know and accept this pattern as pretty normal, especially as it seemed to be replicated by many of the other big families we knew. Sometimes we would sigh and moan, especially if it meant forsaking cartoons on the black-and-white television on the back porch, but mainly we accepted that this was just part of the way we lived our family life.

It was she who took charge of my sacramental journey as an infant in a cold Warwickshire church over half a century ago. Here I was baptised into a family of faith; an act for which I hope to be eternally grateful. I was off to a convent school at Prep and by Grade Two I knew my prayers and my saints and was ready for my First Holy Communion. We children understood that this was a really big step in our faith journey, although we didn't understand the theology of transubstantiation. We knew that our reception of the host was the most important thing and there was much cleaning of teeth and nervous tiny tongues on the big day. I still have the black-and-white photo of a happy, freckled, chubby, buck-toothed child, veil askew, beaming at the camera. I also have my certificate, lovingly written by one of the older FCJ sisters in gold calligraphy. And I still remember the treat of jelly slices at the morning breakfast afterwards!

Confession was a bit of a scary sacrament in the old days. Reconciliation has a much more restorative and holistic feeling about it. My mother would pile us into the car and take us to church to confess the venial sins of dobbing, pinching (sisters, and someone else's prized purple Derwent pencil) and impure thoughts. Everything was on my conscience. Small excusable failings were transmogrified into giant moral lapses and sometimes I had to invent some generic sinfulness if the litany of failings did not seem quite long enough. The one-size-fits-all sin of being rude to my parents was a useful last-minute addition in exchange for absolution. After a short penance of three Hail Marys and a 'Glory Be' I felt good with God again.

For Confirmation, I took my mother's name, Barbara, because I loved her and because Saint Barbara had an exotic life and a gruesome end. Amongst my peers there were lots of Marys and Margarets and Thereses and Bernadettes, so I was also happy that my name was a bit different and not one of the usual sanctified suspects. This sacrament meant that I was fully cognisant of what I was doing. My faith was no longer simply inherited. I was making a confirmed choice to be a Catholic. Looking back, I may have simply been a biddable, believing child and happy to follow through the sacramental journey mapped out for me. I have never looked back.

I believe in the sacrament of marriage. It is a holy state, even though it can be hard work and have its peaks and troughs, its joys and sorrows, its domestic sameness and enduring love, its colourful family life. For me, it means there is an extra element of love in this relationship, God's love. It's another iteration of the eternal triangle, the sacramental version. My husband, who is not a Catholic but a pretty good Protestant, sometimes thinks he's lucky he's married to me, not because I am a domestic goddess or homemaker extraordinaire but simply because he knows that I am in the marriage for life. He jokes he has a life sentence with me. He has!

Saint Augustine wrote, 'The spiritual virtue of a sacrament is like light; although it passes among the impure, it is not polluted'.

We are flawed human beings and we fail often. But when we partake of the sacramental life, especially the Eucharist, we are brought again into the light of God's love. We are raised up, given the chance to try again, a redeeming opportunity to feel good with ourselves and good with God again.

*He will cover you with his feathers
and under his wings you will find refuge.*

PSALM 91:4

Sunday morning at the local café with friends. We enjoy our scrambled eggs and coffee, but we only have an hour for a quick catch up. One friend is off to Mass in Box Hill as he is rostered on to do the readings. I am off to sit quietly in the third from back row in Surrey Hills.

All over Melbourne people are going to Mass. Despite the low attendance and the pontifications that religion is increasingly irrelevant in a secular pluralist age, there is still something heartening in seeing the very old and very young and all ages in-between participating in communal worship. This is the grace and glue of a worshipping community, the identification with a belief that moves beyond the self as centre of the universe. I see a grey-haired couple kiss each other joyfully at the sign of peace, and strangers clasp others' hands warmly. There's a dad who reminds me of my brother. He has a number of tousled haired boys in his care and he answers their sing-song questions about standing and sitting with the patience of a saint. A big Italian family arrives, with model wives and shaggy looking uncles in shades and beaming grandparents wearing discreet gold, all getting ready for a baptism after Mass. The baby is sheathed in taffeta with a pearly headband fixed above a sweet little cherub face. A lovely lady in green hands out the leaflets and has a pleasant word to say to all and sundry. One of the altar servers comes up to chat to me because she has seen me around school and knows that I'm not really the ogre of torrid teacher tales exchanged breathlessly at recess. The woman behind me is a friend of my sister's. A friend and her husband take up their usual seats across the aisle. She will later lead the Prayers of the Faithful as we ask the Lord to hear us.

I am clad in a serviceable pair of leggings and runners and a good long coat. My hair needs a wash and my make-up has been applied hastily and I've got my backpack with me, full of corrections and the bones of an article on poetry I've been trying to finish for weeks. I am not quite invisible, but happy not to be front and centre, just a woman in the third from back row who has her own thoughts and prayers and preoccupations.

One of my favourite hymns is 'Come as You Are'. It's a hymn about God's mercy and forgiveness. It's a hymn of the level playing field, where all our human foibles and frailties are recognised and we come just as we are to worship. There is no hierarchy, no labelling, no judgement, just unlimited love. In some ways we are at our Sunday best (if not always dressed as such in the new casualisation of attire) because we are not dressed in our weekday worries, not networking or having to make a good impression, not competing for promotion or making hard decisions. We are stripped of artifice and the need for recognition because we are brought back to the spiritual basics; we are all loved equally as children of God.

At Mass, we can wash off some of the weekday dust and detritus. We come as we are and are cleansed by new thoughts. Perhaps it is the gospel reading, the well-honed homily, the reception of the Eucharist, the time – a brief hour – spent in God's house. We leave Mass hopeful that we can do and be better the following week.

Occasionally I go to St Francis' in town. Here the unity and diversity of God's people can be witnessed in dreadlocked backpackers, families of all shapes and sizes and nationalities, Sunday shoppers, tourists, those who stay for Mass, those who pop in to light a candle in the Ladye Chapel, those who hover in the foyer, those who contribute what they can to the collection, those dressed up for a matinee, those who doze in the back rows, those who just want to catch their breath in a space that excludes no one. It is a safe haven in a busy metropolis, a place to be in your everyday attire, with your everyday worries and everyday hopes. It is a church that turns no one away; and for those on the street outside its railings begging, it is a refuge and sanctuary away from the grinding hustle of simply staying alive in a big city that feels increasingly impersonal with its concrete canyons and shiny skyscrapers.

St Francis', a walk-in work-a-day church in the middle of the CBD where Ned Kelly's parents were married and Mary MacKillop was baptised and thousands have paused and prayed and pondered. Its doors are open to all. Within, there is an unconditional invitation from God who is always pleased to see you – just as you are.

And thus ever by day and night, under the sun and under the stars, climbing the dusty hills and toiling along the weary plains, journeying by land and journeying by sea, coming and going so strangely, to meet and to act and react on one another, move all we restless travellers through the pilgrimage of life.

CHARLES DICKENS

In the Middle Ages the idea of a pilgrimage was to travel to a shrine or renowned place of worship to ask for help or seek repentance for sins. This journey was usually undertaken on foot, in a group, and is well documented via the colourful characters found in Chaucer's *The Canterbury Tales* as they travel from London to visit the tomb of Saint Thomas à Beckett. John Bunyan, in his fifteenth century tale *A Pilgrim's Progress*, charts the character Christian's eventful journey to the celestial city. In many faith traditions the idea of pilgrimage is one that offers a journey; a spiritual adventure taken on a quieter plane than most adventures, but equally thrilling and life changing.

Those who may not adhere to a religious framework make personal pilgrimages where they commune with nature. Many of those who walk the Camino, recently popularised by the film *The Way*, are looking for meaning beyond their own lived experience. In the simple act of walking, they are noticing things, feeling sun on skin and seeing the changing features of the landscape. Perhaps digital activity has been abandoned, or at least limited, so that there is no blurring of the connection between walker and wilderness. They are looking for more; a more that may provide answers to the big questions.

A pilgrimage is ultimately a journey to self; an awakening journey, sometimes a walking back to happiness or a recalibration of contentment lost in the cut and thrust of twenty-first century living and its demands to be available and accountable and across everything 24/7. This finding of the true self often means discovery and disclosure. It may be the admission of things that do not normally see the light, perhaps things so well hidden that their excavation is confronting. Introspection may unearth unexpected findings and feelings.

A pilgrim is a seeker after truth; the truth held within both sacred places and the secret places we seldom enter. True pilgrimage is transformative. It unlocks the spirit held within us. Sometimes pilgrimage is about listening to the sounds of silence; the sounds that our own hearts sing when away from the hurly-burly of daily life. This is the song true and untroubled, no false notes or jarring chords. In this retreat from life where things are often magnified and success is measured on a scale of excess, where extroversion is an extreme sport and introversion is sidelined as a sad second, silence is as refreshing as strong soaking rain after drought. Pilgrimage is about finding a quiet zone; about honouring reflection and contemplation, reverie and rumination, about the gentle scenic path that travels alongside the gridlocked highway.

Recently I have taken my own small pilgrimages to places that are holy to me. I have a vague map with the key destination – heaven – plotted in, but I know that this map is still being shaded in with the bright colours of discovery and the cool colours of hurt. Although I am most decidedly on a path there are still surprises and joys and disconcertings that will pop up to strengthen and challenge me. I may well be tested and there may be bends in the road when I cannot see what is ahead of me, or forks, or faint trails. I may have to retrace my steps to gain a surer foothold.

An hour's bus ride from the end of the A Line in Rome is the lovely medieval town of Genazzano. Here there is a special church dedicated to Our Lady of Good Counsel. The miracle of a flying fresco of the Madonna and child took hold of my heart when I attended the school of the same name in suburban Kew. Enraptured with the piety of a girl who internalised without question all the stories of the saints, I was immersed into the reality of fabulous founding fables and the mystical world of apparitions and visitations. And so, a lifelong ambition was born. I knew that one day I would visit this sacred place.

Plain from the outside, the interior of the church was stunning, full of gilt and ebonised wood, large devotional paintings and marble statues. These are the gifts of unknown artists who understood the peasant heart that needed to kneel and pray before beauty; the peasant heart that had to feel its way towards a hope that lifted them from the hard reality of struggling and cheerless lives. I particularly loved the exquisitely sculpted altar cherubs who looked as though they had been up to some mischief and had momentarily stopped playing.

The icon is tiny. It has none of the obvious splendour of a Raphael or Murillo in its depiction of loving maternity. Mary is plain and the baby Jesus a chubby bubby with a wizened face who tugs at his mother's garment. However, its importance is not in the artistic aesthetic, but in its meaning for those who venerate it. There is beauty in this evocation of the blessed union of mother and child; and more especially for Catholics who understand the eternity written in this special narrative.

Whenever I think of Our Lady of Good Counsel, I think of that mould-breaking woman of history, the peasant girl Mary who lived two millennia ago in an ancient Palestine administered by the Romans. Mary took the huge risk of love in her fearless fiat to Gabriel's annunciation that she would bear a child. And I also think of other ladies of good counsel, often religious sisters, who have also taken risks in their daring to live a different sort of life. I have the utmost respect and admiration for those women who choose to live in ways that defy the easy and complacent; those women who venture beyond the comfort zones of our material age and journey to help the globally poor in far-off countries; those women who go out into deep water beyond the safety of the shoreline that keeps most of us confined.

I had to see for myself the place after which the school was named – a visit to satisfy my curiosity and embed my understanding of how a school in colonial Victoria could have possibly been named after a small village in Lazio, Italy. In fact, a number of popes have visited Genazzano because of its worship of Our Lady and its many Marian shrines. Saints, too, have knelt here in front of this modest picture: Saint John Bosco, Saint Vincent Palotti, Saint Clement Hoffbauer and the Augustinian priest Blessed Stephen Bellesini whose remains are in a glass coffin in a modern chapel and who died of typhoid fever whilst ministering to victims of the plague. Genazzano is also the birthplace of Pope Martin V, whose papacy effected the end of the Western Schism at the Council of Constance in 1417 and brought about the end of the almost seventy-year Avignon papacy.

So I kneel before the icon and say a couple of cover-note prayers for family and friends. I am an inveterate lighter of candles in churches, a devotional habit I learnt from my pert and pious grandmother Greta. Under the star-spangled ceiling of the Ladye Chapel at St Francis' in Melbourne's CBD, I would imagine the millions of prayers and special intentions that had been sent heavenward on those fierce little flickers of flame. Later, I would wonder if there was an appropriate ecclesial name for this iron contraption which looked more like an Inquisitorial instrument of torture. Here at Genazzano, however, the wax tradition has waned and in a nod to an encroaching health and safety paradigm the candles are now all electric. No acrid little stubs on which to float my hope. Still the intention is there, even if it is all a little safe and colourless with that bit of devotional theatre relegated to the past.

Genazzano is a lovely small town with its medieval arch, well-worn buildings and old-fashioned streetlamps, its alleys decorated with householder pot plants and old wooden shutters open to the sun. It has the rich but unpretentious patina of old Italy and one can imagine in the sleepy lassitude of a warm afternoon that the centuries are no longer numbered and that time stands still. There may be modernisation, but it is well hidden in these terracotta hills.

It is a miracle that we actually got back to the train in one piece. Our bus driver – young, handsome and careless – went careering down the hairpin bends with suicidal speed as he conducted an animated conversation on his handheld mobile with the other hand on the roulette, I mean driver's, wheel. Even the locals began yelling *basta!* – enough! He may have known every stone in the road, but we did not, and it was terrifying. Prayers of gratitude were said as we alighted at Anagnina – and a few other words exchanged too, although they were probably lost in translation and perhaps not of the sanctified variety.

Sometimes I wonder if I have become something of a pilgrimage junkie – what with my self-starting spiritual sabbaticals, my yen and yearning for new ways into my own interior landscape and my delight in nestling into the many and varied founding stories of faith. Perhaps they have become survival tactics in a world that can sometimes be bruising in its unforgiving speed; perhaps they offer me the slower joys of solace and a further robustness for the fray beyond. I joke to my friends that sometimes I visit so many churches that it all becomes a bit of a stained-glass blur – but I wouldn't have it any other way. I would hate anyone to think that I am trying to be *holier than thou*, but we all find avenues to spiritual growth and this seems to do the trick for me. Perhaps I am still in thrall to all the stories of my childhood faith, which is, still and ever, my adult faith. I love adding new shades and nuances and colours to an ever-expanding cavalcade of saints and their weird and wonderful stories that continue to give me ballast in a busy world.

In Lourdes I have never felt more at home in my faith than I did with thousands of other pilgrims singing 'Ave Maria' under the gaze of the Pyrenees. We were one people, from different nations, all believing the same thing … and it was beautiful. I witnessed the best miracle of all – human hope – as I saw men and women of all ages wheeled and carried and pushed to the water, by other men and women of all ages. This was love. And yes, I brought home some holy water for my mother and some magnets for the fridge and I still have my processional candle as a reminder of that night of faith aflame in the French countryside.

And I have been but one of thousands squashed into St Peter's Square, thrilled to see in the distance the tiny figure of Pope Benedict and to feel a great surge of belonging as people waved banners excitedly, cried and felt at home in their faith. Truly, we are a pilgrim church on earth.

Little serendipities make such a difference as we

travel. Joy becomes the breath we take as we wander and wonder and thank God for this time out that dusts off the routine and encourages revelation. Ordinary moments are gilded with the intersections of hope and happiness. The soul is enlarged with new shapes and colours. Grace notes of kindness and companionship and unexpectedness herald the acknowledgement that we all have different spiritual journeys to make, unique to our faith experience and upbringing.

Saint Augustine wrote that 'the world is a book and those who do not travel read only a page'. It seems I have become an avid reader as I sojourn here and there, a pilgrim keen to find new places in my heart, new ways of looking and being, alive and alert to the wonders around me.

Mostly home now, I store up the memories in my mind of all the people and places elsewhere that tell me who I am. I thank God for the plain sailing of the known and the surprises of the unknown and set my course for further adventures of body and soul.

I am no longer lying low.

We are all but travellers here.

SAINT MARY OF THE CROSS MACKILLOP

It was a strangely serendipitous spelling error in a Year 9 student's PowerPoint presentation on Mary MacKillop that got me thinking about what we do, daily, in Catholic schools. The dear girl had been talking about the teenage Mary being the soul (instead of sole) provider for her family. As a stationery clerk growing up in 1850s Melbourne, it had fallen on her young shoulders to look after the family financially as her father's income and employment were erratic. Mary's legacy of charity really did begin at home.

Ever the English teacher, I was straight onto it and commended her inadvertent error which opened up, for me, a whole new way of looking at what Catholic educators do. I joked that she almost deserved an extra mark as this word, soul, was absolutely spot on for an RE class.

We have internet providers and service providers and health providers, all sorts of providers that cater for our material needs, but where do we find soul providers in a world that sometimes seems spiritually barren?

Prayer is one such avenue of provision, a means of nourishment, a well that never runs dry. It is a welcome ritual at the commencement of an RE lesson, some few privileged minutes that allow time for some internal quietness in a world that is demanding and clamorous. It is our opening up to God and I explain the Sign of the Cross as a symbol of readiness and receptivity. It must be executed reverently, not casually. We are then oriented, albeit briefly, to the sacred, before the business of timetable changes, choir rehearsals, debating meetings and lost property announcements.

I love that the students pray for each other unselfconsciously, collectively and with a communal warmth that translates into more than a lovely wish that things get better. A child can share their concerns or hurts or joys. They can pray for victory at netball or for those suffering the torments of natural disasters or terrorism in faraway lands. They can count their daily blessings of good health, play lunch and knowing they sleep safely at night. They can pray for an ill grandparent or a brother on his birthday. The 'Lord hear our prayer' chorused response of the twenty-five others who have witnessed this small petition is charged with an other-worldly grace.

Education is about so much more than literacy and numeracy and becoming a productive economic unit. It is also about soul-searching and finding. Prayer can provide a new learning about self when ego is left behind and silence embraced and we wait for an inner whisper. The beauty of prayer is that the opening of our hearts is as natural as the opening of a flower, wrote the Benedictine priest John Main.

If the young people who share our lives are enabled to appreciate beautiful words and melodies, to see the poetry in a tree and magic in the moon, to hear the ancient swell of the sea in a shell and the sun setting fire to the horizon at the end of the day and to thank God for this, then their souls are nourished indeed.

Individually and institutionally, we can be transformative in the lives of those we teach. And in the gentle and faithful and sometimes robust handling of the bodies and souls sitting in front of us we create and recreate the soul of the Church. On a daily basis, I help to educate well over a hundred girls and hope that a little of what I do or say takes seed. It may be but a momentary interaction; a few words, an idea, an affirmation or acknowledgement, a feeling of solidarity or common purpose, but it can have an impact that lasts well beyond the sixty-five-minute lesson. My soul, as well as my body, is in harness to a greater cause. As well as mandated skills and curriculum knowledge, I share who I am with those I teach.

As an English teacher, my girls know about the three Ps: punctuate, proofread and polish, and the necessity for conforming to convention – in most cases. However, I exhort them to experiment with words and ideas and to defy the unforgiving constraints of the class assessment word count if they have something important to say. As an RE teacher, I also hope to create an environment where the girls feel they have something important to say about who they are and how they find the world around them and what they can offer in the way of goodness to each other and to God. It is in the richness of these permissions that we teachers enable new growth, new blooms coming from the soil of tradition.

I believe that the psychological good that prayer does complements its spiritual dimension. We hear much about bullying in all its insidious manifestations. Class prayer helps provide something of a protective factor that counteracts a pervasive culture that demeans and detracts from the dignity of the person. This is not to say that mean things do not happen, but we are all made aware that we are hoping for behaviours that are tender and merciful; that the bruises and burdens of life are dealt with compassionately; that our souls need nurturing, not haphazardly or as a by-product of the system, but deliberately and purposefully.

I am thrilled that in a small way I can do my bit as

a soul provider. There won't be a measurable outcome for what I do. My input cannot be assessed or evaluated, quantified or dissected – and that's as it should be. Sometimes I'll get through; often I won't. But the soul is too special to be subject to any temporal bureaucracy or the claustrophobic calibrations of a data-driven society.

For each child in front of me, their soul has its own unique and divine imperative. That I may assist on their journey to faith, or self, or to a Eureka moment, or simply add a wondrous new word to the adolescent vocabulary, is what gives a steady singing joy to this old soul.

But words are things, and a small drop of ink,
Falling like dew, upon a thought, produces
That which makes thousands, perhaps millions, think.

LORD BYRON

My resolution this year is to acquaint my students with the joys and poetry of the collective noun. So scared am I that we are losing the language battle that I am going to institute some fun and games into the lower secondary classroom. Teenagers will be going home to alert, but not alarm, their parents that the collective noun for rattlesnakes is rhumba. They will find out that tiding is the collective noun for magpies.

We all know about a murder of crows (create own

footy joke here) and a pride of lions and a kindle, clutter, glaring or clowder of cats. Don't we?

In the years of my Victorian education in the early 1970s, not the *fin de siècle*, my good teachers gave us lists. Lists of synonyms and antonyms, spelling lists, lists of collective nouns, lists of the weird words, -ology words, occupation words, lists for almost everything. They were times tables for words, a bit of muscular word building and our vocabularies were all the richer for it. In the twenty-first century will our children's vocabularies be the equivalent of Neanderthal grunts and a digital patois of emoticons and *txt*?

Am I alone here in hoping that our language will not become so betrothed to technology that the words of wonder and wisdom, of arcane and mysterious etymological provenance, die a quick and fairly painless death on the altar of apps? Will the words of the poets be sacrificed to the casualisation of the language, all but disembowelled by the numerate nerds and programmers of Silicon Valley? Will collective nouns become a curiosity, housed in a display case of the past, a museum piece for future generations, something shelved in the archives of the human story?

A murmuration of starlings – doesn't that just sing of poetry? A blessing of unicorns – medieval myths and chivalrous knights and great ladies at court? A shrewdness of apes. A fluther or smack of jellyfish. Or that fantastical, dark, glowering, portentous, unkindness of ravens. What of a piteousness of doves which sounds rather more evocative than the more commonly used dole or flight?

What does an ambush of widows suggest? A superfluity of nuns? A tabernacle of bakers? How fabulous an implausibility of gnus or a sleuth of bears. What fun a mischief of mice must have under the floorboards after we have retired for the night.

Clever punnings also provide new collective nouns. In an episode of Inspector Morse, the great detective mused as to what the possible collective noun was for pathologists. Of course – body. More recent collective nouns include an audit of accountants, a brace of dentists, a squint of proof-readers, a ponder of philosophers and one I particularly like, a logorrhoea of lexicographers.

I'll ask my students to come up with new collective nouns as they moan that this must be some new torture devised by the torment of teachers they have this year who will no doubt give them a slew of homework. They'll enrol their parents to come up with clever ideas and thus the language will grow. They will wade into the warm water of words, no longer afraid of the new or the long or the unusual or the phonetically difficult. Shakespeare invented words to suit his occasion and Lewis Carroll threw off the shackles of convention for a bit of jabberwocky. We should encourage this language evolution, despite the education revolution of more computers and school halls, league tables and bureaucratic babels.

I have been having my own fun with collective nouns these holidays. A garrulity of grandmothers, a disorder of drunkards, a condescension of waiters, a skirmish of siblings, a pedantry of proofreaders and I can be rightfully accused, given the nature of this article, of belonging to that rather odd but gentle group, a whimsy of writers.

Meanwhile I am waiting for the parliament – of owls – to join with the party of rainbow fish, the coalition of cheetahs, the labour of moles, the congress of baboons and the buffoonery of orangutans with their excuses – I mean, vagary of impediments – to lend some added colour to our collective lives this year.

This is an edited version of an article previously published in *The Age*, March 2017.

Delicious autumn! My soul is wedded to it and if I were a bird I would fly above the earth seeking successive autumns.

GEORGE ELIOT

Autumn and the falling leaves turn footpaths into slippery russet runways. A new colour range is seen in parks and gardens and on the slopes of distant hills. Trees have shed the fulsome foliage of brighter days. Old gold and deep crimson become the gilded shades of nature's palette. The sun becomes a distant pearl hiding behind a blurry gauze of cloud.

As summer slips away to the northern hemisphere the warmth and refuge of home is sought more eagerly. The football and netball seasons add a full-voiced tribalism to our weekends and we know again the elation of muddy victory and the despair of a one-point loss. The eccentric tattoos of our football heroes are on display, musculature masquerading as art form. We don warmer clothes, layering our looks to wrap up against the weather. We are readying ourselves for a change in demeanour, a little more time spent indoors, time for reverie and rumination, an adaptation that prioritises the interior. We are pausing, changing gear, discerning a different rhythm to our days.

Birds still sing in trees but their song is less constant and chirrupy; their chirp has become a little more classical, no longer the heavy rock of summer, but songs with spaces and silences in them. The sky is no longer bathed in blue, but is now a glimmery grey. The St Kilda foreshore is depopulated and stores are stocking up with coats and doonas and supplies of hearty comfort food. It is time to taste the earth's bounty in food from a farmer's market, linger over lunch, enjoy the close bosoming of family and friends.

In literature, autumn is often associated with the downhill run of life, but this overlooks the season as one of celebratory completion; the success of summer has given way to the richness of autumnal reward. Time is ripe with recognition, of good times past and good things ahead.

It is time to gather in the harvest of the years.

I may well be in the early autumn of my days as

pilgrim on Earth, but I can still feel summer in my skin. I am not yet thinking of bucket lists, but of life lists and the gathering of the people and purposes around me that colour my life richly. I am not quite ascetic or holy enough not to want to have a few material goods that are my own special heirlooms; family treasures that speak of what matters to me – the portraits of my father and mother; my grandmother's Victorian Madonna and Child sculpture; black-and-white photos of my siblings as we grew up; some trinkets from travels, a couple of good paintings and beloved books, my daughter's handmade birthday cards. So while I am looking ahead, still working and dreaming with plans to hatch and places to go, I am also reminiscing, harvesting time and memory and wisdom in words and pictures that sing of a life lived gratefully.

I still have much to do in the story of my life.

I seem to be reflecting more on what it means to live this good life. I like to think that I am wising up; that the later, riper years are bearing a new sort of fruit. Some nights before I retire I do the Examen, not always very well, but I sit in my grandmother's chair in the lounge room with the light off and the gentle exhalations of the day cocooning me. I think over my day, where I did well and where I could have done better, and thank God for the morrow to try again.

Autumn is the season for measured walks and slow perambulations; for mooching and meandering and mellowing; for noticing the changes in the air as leaves dance and swirl in suburban streets and children hurry home from school. It is the time for lingering, rather than rushing, for time unspooling gently in the company of loved ones; a season for reminiscence and reunion. It is a season of kindness and kith and kin, homemade hand-knits and woolly mittens and the nourishing broth of togetherness. Jack Hibberd wrote: 'Melbourne in Autumn. Mellow yet crisp. The occasional keen wind. Good for the nerve ends' (*A Toast to Melba*, 1975).

As we immerse ourselves in the alleluia of autumn we respond to the offerings of the season. We weave its slower joys and sometimes moody onslaughts into the sheltering patchwork of our days. As the wind scuffles behind us and the slate grey sky lowers above us, we are reminded that 'For everything there is a season, and a time for every matter under heaven' (Ecclesiastes 3:1).

I'm just going to write because I cannot help it.

CHARLOTTE BRONTË

9.23 pm. Saturday. Balmy April evening. Ten literature essays corrected, nine average, one scatty and brilliant. Handwriting appalling. Spelling phonetic and approximate. Husband snoozing in front of the television as Richmond dies in battle. Daughter snuffling through her dreams. Five essays to go before I can tick the box on *The Great Gatsby* for my seventeen-year-old students and open the ruled notebook that is the reliquary of my ruminations. Continue to check list for punctuation, critical analysis, vocabulary, metalanguage – something I still can't quite grasp. No marks for imagination. I make helpful comments in the margins hoping that they will be read and knowing that this is unlikely. Tutors will tell them the same thing and charge their parents extravagantly for the pleasure. Train in distance. Possums in foreground. Not unfriendly night sounds. Lilt of neighbour's radio, muted rock 'n' roll through double brick walls. Subterranean whisperings, pipes talking, toilets flushing, daddy long legs crouching in dim corners, motes of moon dust hover, invisible cosmic confetti, silvering silhouettes. Kitchen clock ticking. Digital clock flashing. Time passing. My turn.

Saturday night at the kitchen table, the workbench of my dreams, the green light at the end of my dock, the hope of …

The words wait in the wings, occasionally arriving on cue; their stage, my page. Sometimes they glide on effortlessly, a bravura performance when imagination and vocabulary somehow transcend the more prosaic rumblings of creative effort. Sometimes a phrase is whispered to me from the gods and I grab it greedily for fear it will vanish before I can write it down. Sometimes my words skitter and dance before me, beautiful and crazy, and I wonder if I could have possibly imagined them into existence. Other times the clunk clunk clunk of the mundane, the merely competent, becalms me and I am stuck wordless. And clueless.

I write because I must, but my words will not feed me, so our assignation takes place in stolen moments; odd hours at night, the brief sojourn at a café on the way to work, the occasional afternoon when my daughter is with friends, the booking of a small room at Balwyn Library most Sunday afternoons or a trip into the State Library during the holidays. Sometimes I cannot sleep trying to think of plots and character names and an opening sentence that will equal Daphne du Maurier's 'Last night I dreamt I went to Manderley again' (*Rebecca*, 1938) or L.P. Hartley's 'The past is a foreign country: they do things differently there' (*The Go-Between*, 1953). I read reviews and imagine writing festivals and make lists of books I must read, but never get to. I forage delightedly in the work of old and unfashionable writers like J.B. Priestley and Elizabeth Taylor (not the actress). I have recently loved reading *The Elegance of the Hedgehog* by Muriel Barbery and *The Consolations* by Anna Gavalda and have just finished reading Carson McCullers' *The Ballad of the Sad Café*, first published in 1953. I am now in the middle of Tim Winton's *The Boy Behind the Curtain* and I love the invitational ease and familiarity of his writing and his deep love of landscape. My reading life is random and episodic. Occasionally, I'll read the latest bestseller or Booker or Pulitzer, but more often than not it is a book that has had its day, but still has something to say. Penelope Lively's *Moon Tiger* is a recent favourite, as are John Banville's *The Sea* and Siri Hustvedt's *What I Loved*. And the ten years it took Anthony Doerr to write *All the Light We Cannot See* was absolutely worth it. I have just read Sally Rooney's *Normal People* and remember the ache and drama of first love, the secrets and lies and doubts and dizziness and the trust implicit in giving away your heart to someone else's keeping. It seems the past is really a different country – or perhaps we write in generational ways where for those of a certain age the love scene is finished with the close-up and fade-out of the kiss and the rest is left to the imagination. There is no mystery in the explicit.

I write out words and phrases and beautiful sentences so that they can work their magic on me. I make plans to read the great classics that I have overlooked, something by Turgenev perhaps, but know that I will never get to them either and that somehow a little overlooked gem, picked up at a local fete, something by Anna Quindlen or Julian Barnes, will ease that pain. I dream of unfettered time to myself where I can sit and read for three hours and not feel guilty that I am not busying myself more purposefully.

8.47 pm. Sunday. Just tuning into *Downton Abbey*. Work tomorrow. The journeyman day of instruction and exchange where my words become less glittering and fold into the functionality of pedagogy. My imagination is temporarily suspended, sidelined for the next six days, importuned to the business of employment.

Notebook closed. Dreams on hold.

On that best portion of a good man's life,
His little, nameless, unremembered, acts
Of kindness and of love.

WILLIAM WORDSWORTH

My father was the deep anchor of the family. A bookish medical man, we seven little Australians often thought he would have made a good priest because he was so interested in theology and Church issues. He was an avid reader and letter writer to *The Advocate* and to state politicians and premiers. On his desk stood a bust of Daniel Mannix, the influential archbishop of Melbourne. The Irish prelate lived till ninety-nine, opposed conscription and walked to St Patrick's Cathedral from his home at Raheen in Kew until well into his eighties. My father admired his courage and conviction in those old days when Catholics took their lead from the diocesan pulpit. Books about religion and ethics, true crime and the odd political biography littered my father's study. He was keen on the two Bobs, Santamaria and Hawke. I never saw him read a novel.

My mother was the one who supervised prayers and went through the catechism questions and made sure we went to confession on a fairly regular basis. Here we'd own up to pinching a sibling or four, fibbing to Mother about completing homework or having mean thoughts about the girl in class who possessed the elegant Derwent set of twenty-four pencils while we made do with the small stubby six-pack of primary colours from Coles. But it was my father who gave each of us twenty cents to put on the plate. It was he who quietly sent money to the missions in India. It was he who believed in the birth right of every child. It was he who worked hard to put us to Catholic schools because he came from old school Irish stock and believed in the faith of the fathers. It was he who was black and white on some issues and guided by his conscience on others.

His was the quiet plateau of work as I grew up; sometimes a father on the sidelines, so busy was he with being the breadwinner and father to me and my six siblings. He made other men fathers by delivering their infants safely into waiting arms. He watched over me, provided for me, loved me. He checked my secondary school essays and was proud of my efforts. He was a clear thinker in a world of spin where words are tortured into meaninglessness by those who would lead us astray. He was a man who loved liquorice and jazz piano and his children. He was a man who enjoyed the TV series *Colombo*, swam twenty lengths doggedly every day and was faithful to the Church. He was a man who did the right thing even when people weren't looking. He was an honourable man. He was a man who let my mother do the talking, with her amusing and occasionally tart loquacity, unless he had something to say.

In the film *Bend It Like Beckham*, Jess's mother, Mrs Bhamra, famously notes that children are a map of their parents. And so we are, unless we choose to negotiate a different terrain or reject that map as a cartographical relic and of little use in a world where we now have GPS and a digital footprint to define and locate us. My father was a thinker whose reading material was often biblical. He was interested in Judaism, often buying or ordering books to further his knowledge. He wanted to know about Jesus of Nazareth and how this humble carpenter, from an imperial backwater in the Roman Empire, changed the world.

My father was a man of faith. I am his daughter. The map has changed slightly in the inevitability of generational and social shift, but I have not lost my way. I thank God for my father who without fuss or bother quietly supported me and perhaps, because I was his first child, favoured me a little. I have a small portrait of him in my lounge room, a Meldrumesque tribute by my aunt to her brother who probably sat impatiently for her, as the brushstrokes are full and loose, rather than tightly precise. He is still watching over me. Sometimes I'll exchange the odd word with him about the world and its ways, an almost prayerful offering to this quiet man who shaped much of my life. I'll be grateful for the qualities and attitudes that are lived out through his children, my siblings, the ordinary decencies and daily goodness that undergird all they do. My father was the least judgemental man I have ever known and I never heard him say a bad word about anyone. He was implacably loyal.

All fatherhood is shaped differently through the domestic intangibles and intimacies of family life. There are dads helping with homework, dads at the footy, dads picking up the partying teenagers at one in the morning; dads listening and laughing; dads telling lame dad jokes and being totally embarrassing; dads at the parish working bee or on the parent council; dads working all hours for the love of their own holy rollicking untamed families; working, providing, supporting; being there. Sometimes CEO of the couch, occasionally backyard inventor, often the backbone of the family unit, frequently BBQ king.

The next generation of fathers will be more hands-on. They will cook and clean and nurse as some of their wives take on the job that pays better and he goes to toddler gym classes or reads the bedtime story. This new family narrative may be written with different expectations. Perhaps the old paradigm of the greed and strut that was part of the male work trajectory will be softened by part-time work that enables families to function more healthily. There will be a fairer division of labour and a slow dismantling of the gendered jobs of the past. There will be some negotiating in this new age, but the gifts of fatherhood will become even more apparent. Fathers who say 'thank you', do the vacuuming and model the best of what it is to be masculine will pass this onto their own children, especially their boys. They will not see it as emasculating to do the ironing as their wives mow the lawn, nor will they have to keep a stiff upper lip when their hearts are breaking. Perhaps there will be a revised recognition that a man's heart can break too and that to show emotion is not weakness.

All fathers are different. Their role as father is unique and irreplaceable. They will pass on the best of what it is to be a man, just as they pass on life lessons, the actions and stories of faith as well as who their progeny will spend a lifetime barracking for in a city whose other religion is AFL. The parental map will make its inimitable mark genetically, but also in attitudes, actions, gestures and vocabulary, that strange familial minutiae that threads its way through the generations.

Let us also remember all those who father even if

not in a biological sense. It is those good men who counsel, mentor and laugh, who know when to say something and when to refrain. They may be uncles or teachers or priests or family friends or sports coaches; other good guys who know the value of encouragement and advice, especially for young men negotiating the difficult terrain of growing up into the men we want and need them to be.

There is in souls a sympathy with sounds:
And as the mind is pitch'd the ear is pleased
With melting airs, or martial, brisk or grave;
Some chord in unison with what we hear
Is touch'd within us, and the heart replies.

WILLIAM COWPER

I have always loved the hymn 'Amazing Grace'. I have it at home sung by Elvis and Harry Secombe and Judith Durham. Although each version is sung differently according to vocal register and arrangement, it still carries, anthemically and defiantly, its central message of hope. It is a hymn that unites all believers, of whatever persuasion, in the bigger belief that, despite our trials and tribulations, our sins and errings, grace will take us home. It's a hymn that has been around long enough to cater for various interpretations; it's baggy enough for a soulful wail, for the gravelly voice or the thrilling tenor, the jazz singer or the amateur who is all heart. It is a hymn that has crossed mountains and oceans and continents and has found favour with all who have been lost and found.

If my soul is a tiny barque sailing on troubled waters, with occasional becalmings and squally weather, with tempests and tides, and rogue waves and the sometimes glorious propulsion towards my destination when the wind is at my back, my safe harbour will be that final landing place anchored in eternity.

My sister Gel and I sang this beautiful hymn as my father's coffin was wheeled out after his funeral Mass. He had wanted his girls to sing for him this final time and this was our tribute; a tribute to a man who had delivered over three thousand Melbourne babies and who always cherished his privileged role in bringing children into the world. This was a grace bestowed on him every time a child was born.

We did not falter or become teary, although many in the congregation did, because this was his homecoming. As his eldest child, I held it together just as he would have expected me to. The tears come when I least expect them. And we have the legacy of an amazing grace that his children share with each other in a love that is strong and enduring. We have been blessed by the fatherhood of a good man – not perfect – doing his best, earnestly and honestly, and for that we are eternally grateful. It is a grace we could not recognise in those long ago family meals of seven children, Ann, Fiona, Geraldine, Rosemary, Francis, Dominique and Matthew, boisterous and hungry and voluble, who each tried to carve out a bit of attention before our busy parents, our dear Fath and Moth, who are now in heaven. Oh, how grace is weaved inextricably into the threads of life and death; into our own small local stories and into the great heaving waves of history.

It is often hard to apportion influence when it comes to one's parents. My father was one of those quietly honourable men; the ones who do not want or need acclaim, who do the right thing because it is the right thing and not because they might be applauded for it in the public sphere. I know that he delivered babies without charge for young women who might have found themselves 'in trouble', as it was called in the old days. The sacredness of each life, no matter how conceived, was what mattered to him and I was always proud that these quiet actions attested to who he was at heart. He never talked about his growing up, but had a lifelong affection for the Christian Brothers who helped a scholarship boy from working class Middle Park get to St Kevin's and enrol to do medicine at the University of Melbourne. He would admit he had been a terrible swot, always at the books, although I have since seen some teenage photos of him dressed up as a pirate in amateur dramatics and a few black-and-white photos of long-ago medical balls. I think he was the least dramatic person I knew – no nonsense, straightforward, constant, perhaps a bit fuddy-duddy. My mother was the opposite – she was witty, charming, sociable, able to mix and match it with anyone. He would make lists and tick things off and write articles. She would laugh and organise events and read voraciously. His Saturday routine for most of my younger years was a visit to his rooms in East Melbourne, a swim at the Beaurepaire pool at the university and fish and chips in newspaper for the two or three or four of us on the way home. He would drop us to netball games in faraway suburbs and doze behind the Sunday papers in the lounge room. He and my mother would host election parties in the days when one's politics could be discussed with civility and rational debate. He was measured, my mother was mercurial.

Humility is not a quality that gets much press today in a world that demands self-promotion, branding, a constant curation and visibility in the public gaze. It is an old school virtue at odds with the narcissistic individualism and me-ism that turns everything into an opportunity for a photo or a tweet or a hashtag. Sometimes, I wish my father had had a bit more push, as my mother had, but he was always true to his values and was not one to glad handle or be sycophantic as a means of progressing up the ladder. That being said, he once appeared on television in the early seventies, interviewed by Annette Allison about something contentiously medical. He was also an early adopter of technology with his embarrassingly brick-sized Telmar, which invariably went off in Mass much to our chagrin and the priest's annoyance. My father may have seemed to us something of a plodder when put up against the smooth people-pleasing networking types, but he enjoyed the sideshows of the VRC, mooching around bookshops, going for constitutionals in the evening, walking with a stick like a shillelagh and thinking his own thoughts. He was a private man – not one for show or tell.

There is a grace in humility and modesty, in reticence and gentleness. It is the demeanour that listens instead of having to be heard, that notices little things, that believes that effort, regardless of the size of the enterprise, is important and does not always have to be celebrated. Not everything needs approval and approbation and the lauding and applauding that some find as necessary as oxygen. Not everything is about the opening night or the select group, the rich list, the right connections or the best and brightest. Most of us won't make any of those lists, and that is fine. Most of us, ordinary decent people doing our bit where we can, will not be celebrated except by those who know and love us and appreciate what we have really done; the instances where we have chosen others over ourselves or have done something extra because we can. I think of my friends tutoring refugees, doing a weekly stint at Vinnies, volunteering to write for community or in-house magazines, dropping off meals to elderly neighbours. My father did things quietly and without fanfare, the odd shift at Ozanam House and some exchange medical work in Nauru and the United Arab Emirates.

His was the grace of equanimity and acceptance, not bitterness or victimhood, even when passed over for promotion. His was the grace of the long haul and the dedication it took. Not long before he died, he told me that he had few regrets in his life, especially his professional life. There were some personal hurts, but my father never spoke about these. I never heard him bad mouth anyone. He kept things in – part of that generation who did not overshare and thought emotional displays were messy.

My mother was much more emotional. Between the two of them, I have inherited both a work ethic and the liking of a good party. I'm not averse to putting in the hours for something that matters to me. My father would read my articles and wonder about my anecdotal circumnavigations which took forever to get to the point. He liked words to be direct, none of that meretricious embellishment that consumed paragraphs on the page. His feedback was always affirmative, although he would underline in red Texta words or phrases he either liked or wondered about. I was fortunate to benefit from his keen eye for the right word and my mother's delight in words that shone beyond the literal.

We all have gifts and talents passed on through the familial strain. Some will be further refined into prodigy and purpose; others may lapse through disinterest or disuse. I have been graced with a unique combination inherited from my parents. I carry the conundrum, as we all do, of whether nature or nurture has enabled these to become features in my own life. Regardless, I carry on some of the best of my parents and will pass on some of the best of me to my own daughter, Grace, as will my husband. This is the amazing grace of each and every life.

My father was faithful to the end. He got to the finishing line.

He was heading home.

When it comes to life the critical thing is whether you take things for granted or take them with gratitude.

GILBERT KEITH CHESTERTON

Last words, so banal,
Before the chasm that divides before and after.
This world and the next.
Words of glue and grace, of cliché and mumble, and hints to other stories in a wink or a sigh or nod.
Not clever words, or pithy or mystic or odd,
Just the everyday shorthand of the loved familiar.
Anointed with the watery blessing of a slow smile,
For spending a quick half hour with him between

chores on a day off and the load of washing and time to read a book and catching up with a friend and the excuses that eat voraciously into the things that matter.

Those last thirty minutes of love and duty wrapped together in the not knowing of that last time ever.

The gaps of silence and the casual intimacy of father and daughter as the conversation made its usual way;

Enquiries as to daughter, husband, siblings,

Enquiries as to work and long ago friends,

Enquiries as to the world beyond the 5.00 pm dinner of mash and meat for aged gums,

Chewing the fat.

His eighty-five good years and the children – six little Australians and an English honeymoon child – loved in his distant truthful way,

The siblings knotted together in the warm skein of shared history and the fibs and fettlings of time gone by.

A man who knew his God and believed – in his way,

A man who somehow knew the asceticism of the priestly life and thanked the Christian Brothers for the old days, not of strap, but of scholarship,

A man who lived the life he planned and was grateful for the good that came his way.

A man who loved his children,

A man who was our deep anchor in the sometimes rambunctious, chaotic, whirligig madness of seven kids, and measles, and broken hearts, and delivering babies, and doling out pennies for the plate and trying to get a word in at the dinner table, and checking my written words to elicit meaning from the meandering ...

A man.

Who lived his days upon the Earth,

And now lies under it.

A quick half hour visit and the leaving of some favourite biscuits and an article or two cut from the weekend paper that he never got to read,

And the promise to see him next week.

'All the time in the world' he used to say and we would sigh as we rushed to the next thing, importuned by an improvised urgency,

And now we will have all time ...

In the next world.

And so I hold on gratefully to the last words, his benediction to an eldest child,

A 'thank you' and a 'cheerio'.

And that's enough for me.

This is an edited version of an article previously published in *The Record*, St Vincent de Paul Society, July 2018.

And she brought forth her firstborn son, and wrapped him in swaddling clothes, and laid him in a manger; because there was no room for them in the inn.

LUKE 2:7

Over the course of his career my father delivered over three thousand Melbourne babies. He never got over the miracle of birth. A devout man, each squishy squalling baby boy or girl was a unique and wonderful gift from God and he always felt humbled and privileged to help bring a child safely into the world. Growing up we got used to his odd hours and late nights and abandoned cups of tea all around the house because he was so often on call. Babies have a complete and healthy disregard for the timing of their arrival, so cold chops and missing family events and being late to things was the pattern of family life that we seven children knew as normal. At his funeral last year were a number of women whose babies, the first or the fifth or all of them, he had delivered. They remembered his kindness in staying with them all night, especially in the days before the father was welcomed into the maternity suite and the private miracle of birth became a much more public spectacle. My father believed in the blessedness of each and every birth.

When I was about to deliver my first and only child, I had the luxury of five days in hospital, with nurses popping in to check my progress, tasty meals on a platter and a constant stream of visitors joyfully nursing my newborn. Her first home was a tiny white second-hand cradle with lots of bunny-rugs and fluffy toys. Her tiny pink hands and feet were encased in hand-knitted mittens and booties and she was already a fashion victim with her wardrobe of Target 0000 doll size suits for every day of the week. She settled down into the sleep-feed-look-at-the-world routine and my life was to be re-choreographed in unexpected, and usually delightful, ways.

The joy of a firstborn child is world changing. Everything forever is reconfigured; mothers and fathers are made, and their world is never the same again. It is changed again when siblings arrive to add to the colour, clamour and cost, although no price can attend the new love that blooms each time a child is born.

This is the never-ending story of the human family; hope born again each time a new babe takes their first blessed breath of life.

Angels and archangels
May have gathered there,
Cherubim and seraphim
Thronged the air,
But only His mother
In her maiden bliss,
Worshipped the Beloved
With a kiss.

CHRISTINA ROSSETTI

My daughter, Grace, was due on Christmas Day twenty-five years ago, but as is the way with the glorious unpredictable miracle of birth, she stalled her arrival till early January. Like holy Mary, I carried my Grace for nine months and her birth changed forever and immeasurably my identity. She made me a mother.

As the swollen bloom of my pregnancy became apparent, I began to think about the child I would bring into this world. I would look at other pregnant women who, it seemed to me, glowed with an inner serenity, great with expectation. And I would dream of the child within and wish her a love I never knew I possessed. Today as she trembles on the brink of adulthood, I look at her and marvel. Here is the greatest gift of all, my child, who will carry some good into the world. I do not know where her future may take her, but I do know that she has been guided well and that what she does next is hers, and hers alone, to do. In the fullness of time, she will become just the person she was always destined to be.

I wonder what the village girl Mary thought of the child she would deliver. She knew that her child would change the world because Gabriel had told her so, but the repercussions of this holy conception would have been beyond the most tender and profound of her imaginings. She knew, only, that somehow in the vast cosmic design beyond her mortal grasp, all generations would call her blessed. What gracious acquiescence to carry such a divine gift. Did she suffer morning sickness? Would she have felt the leaping in the womb her cousin Elizabeth did? The quickening of life? Did her boy child wriggle in her womb, and kick, and suck his thumb and tire her out as she travelled around Judea?

I imagine Mary, joyful and patient, waiting. A beautiful anticipation mixed with apprehension, as she and Joseph travelled to Bethlehem to be registered under Roman decree. There was no room at the inn, so her child was born in a humble manger with the gentle lowing of cattle a refrain of welcome. Shepherds left their flocks. Star-spangled seraphim serenaded the Saviour. And, as the evangelist Luke tells us, she treasured the angels' words and pondered them in her heart.

I wondered what my child would look like and no imagining could equal the blessing of the tiny, wrinkled bundle with ET eyes and button nose, the fruit of my womb. And I pondered in my heart the miracle of my daughter. My husband, too, was awed and delighted by this little person who would reshape our lives, creating with her birth, a family. Swaddled in fine fleece knitted with grandmotherly love for a new generation she was happy to finally be here, to start her life on Earth, to continue the story of the Irish and the Scottish, the mixed marriages of faith, the blood ties that bind, the skin and skein of another generation. In her story ours would be inextricably entwined, the joyous meshing and overlapping of lives in all their mystery and magic, a new soul emerging from the strange cosmic cauldron from which all generations are brewed into being to name each other loved.

Each time we see a nativity play we see children stepping into this sacred story with delight. There is Mary – from Grade One – serious about her role as mother and ready to do her parents proud. Joseph is one of the older primary school boys, in brown with a false beard and tugging at the cord around his hessian tunic. The three wise men are the school triplets and the real live baby Jesus is a baby that has been borrowed from his family for an hour. He is lying on straw and is swaddled in a nappy and may, just to keep things peaceful, briefly have a dummy in his mouth. As the children present their play and forget lines and cues and somehow do a beautiful job their innocence shines out for all in the audience to see. It is a balm for hearts that have been hardened in the light of the year's disappointments or misgivings. It is a jubilant jolt of joy for those for whom the year has been good. And however the year has panned out with its surprises and duties, its certainties and crestfallings, seeing a nativity play or kneeling in front of a home-grown manger near the altar, we grow into kindness and kinship for those by whom we are surrounded.

The throbbing tug of love between mother and child begins at birth and lasts a lifetime. Mary, too, must have marvelled at her own infant, he of deified destiny, worshipped by those wise men carrying spices from lands faraway. The world is made new when a child is born and we are swaddled again in innocence.

Our weary old planet, fragile and faltering as it spins like a giant gaudy bauble in space, is remade again whenever we celebrate the birth of a child. Joy is shared by grandparents and aunties and neighbours and friends and colleagues and strangers who smile in the street at the newborn babe.

It is a blessing multiplied.

*The hand that rocks the cradle
is the hand that rules the world.*

WILLIAM ROSS WALLACE

A small shaft of guilt unsettles me – briefly – as I plan a day without my daughter. I plan not to see her for five short hours and admit that perhaps she is being short-changed. On a day not yet written on with work or other obligations it could be her turn to have me to herself. Swings and slides in the local park beckon pink skin and jellybean legs to clamber gleefully over their steely structures.

But I have other plans.

My maternal pride observes that the plumpness of babyhood has been forsaken over summer and a growing sturdiness is evidenced in my daughter's five-year-old new Prep limbs. A little girl is emerging – emerging with noise and chatter and shiny bright eyes and a vocabulary that constantly surprises and occasionally disquiets. My baby is growing up. I grasp these gossamer moments greedily while they linger and float in the breeziness of recent memory and then *pop!* into the vapour of the past.

But there is another me and its insistent voice clamours to be heard.

Against the melody of motherhood, it raises its brassy note, a counterpoint to the main composition. Its singular swell cannot simply be subsumed into the larger orchestration. And so, I give voice to that part of me that craves a recognition beyond the reproductive. Perhaps I am trying to reassert my sense of self, trying to be more than simply somebody's mother. Yet in being the mother of my particular somebody, my daughter, Grace, I love and am loved in return.

Mother and child. A simple, sacramental equation; the most beautiful words in the world.

I think of the hours and years my mother spent in simply being *Mummy*. That perhaps in some way she was devoured by the needs and attention we sought, that she only got back to herself when it was almost too late to remember who she was. At night as she listened to those first attempts at reading, did she sometimes drift away, away from nappies and nursery rhymes, to the land before mother time?

Were there times when she was worn out with love?

The creative motherhood of my sisters and friends stand as shining examples of energy and devotion. My younger sister painted and pottered and pottied for hours with her lively brood. She always had the patience and interest to listen to the yelps of delight as chubby fingers grasped paintbrushes clumsily and paint globbed onto smocks and carpet and occasionally adorned butchers' paper. Those reds and blues and violent hues, gruesome eyes and strange body parts were the essence of new discovery. On that simple canvas choices were made and allowed and the world of growing up began to be coloured in. Did it matter that Daddy had green hair and Mummy one long thick black monobrow? Did it matter that noses were missing and the sun was blue? What admiration I hold for my sister who still had the energy and kindness to pack up, wipe down, clean and clear and then provide muffins for morning tea.

Will my daughter accuse me of being less than loving for the sometimes demand of wanting to do my thing instead of her thing? Will she come to understand that her Mummy is special but also fallible? Will she forgive me for the odd days when I have booked her into the holiday program so that I could reclaim a bit of myself, for myself? Will she understand that I had to make some time for me so that I could all the better love her? That the happy me, in following my own small star, would come to her with delight and indulgence, not boredom and irritation?

The past may be another country, but the future is undiscovered terrain. I will make discoveries about myself as mother and she will learn that I am not the same as other mothers. But I won't be embarrassingly different. I'll take my turn on the roster and help where I can. I already know that I am a peanut butter sandwich and sultanas sort of mum. And that the best lunch comes from the tuck shop.

Over the past few months, the kindergarten certainties of finger painting, afternoon naps and well-balanced meals on time have been replaced with the morning rush, notes to be signed, bulletins to be read. Thus we are hurled into an array of activities to acclimatise us to the world of school with its timetables, routines, new friends and other parents. Just last week Gracie celebrated her fifth birthday with fourteen of her *bestest* friends, each of whom wanted desperately to sit next to her. I was proud of my daughter as she laughed and ran and ate too much birthday cake in the excitement of her big day.

In February she received her first Valentine's card, hand delivered by our eight-year-old neighbour and his mother. In March she came third in her running event at the Twilight Sports. Now in April she can write her own name. We wait to see what May brings.

Her first ever school report suggested that she needs to be reminded to pick up after herself. It also said she had made a great start in Prep. For a mother, such confirmation is worth all the cajoling, bribery and insistence that are part and parcel of parental persuasion.

At home Gracie will insist on *helping* me cook, is hooked on *Harry's Practice* and remembers to say thank you most of the time. She can answer the phone with secretarial aplomb, only spits the dummy occasionally, and knows how to smile in such a way that any naughtiness disappears in a cloudburst of love. And she knows the efficiency of small fibs, especially in relation to the cleaning of teeth, washing of hands and saying of prayers.

I witness the small accomplishments that make a mother smile, the staging posts of growth and change. Our children can change the colour of our days and the landscape of our lives. Without fully realising it, they have the power to charge, irrevocably, a moment. In a word or gesture we can be knocked flat by disappointment or elated by prodigy. They stake their claim on our lives; another chapter added to the family narrative, to the works-in-progress that all families are. With six siblings, the story of my family is constantly undergoing revision and the chapters of the past still catch us out in surprise and delight. Sometimes, too, the past can ambush you with the reminders of the small wounds once thought safely swept under the carpet of childhood, only to resurface during the psychological renovation of adulthood.

The way I see, for example, my teenage chapters contrasts markedly with the way my mother sees them.

I wonder how Gracie and I will retell similar tales. I can hear the 'Oh, Mum' already as I embellish a story and she adheres strictly to the facts. Revisionism is not limited to the pages of history. We all tell the family story differently and over the years of retelling and reshaping, editing and adding, it becomes part of the family lore.

Meeting other mothers makes me realise that what I do with my child is not so different. We're all cutting corners, doing the best we can in our circumstances and, mostly, we wouldn't change a thing. We understand our huge responsibility in bringing our children up to be decent human beings, to prepare them to take on the world. And we know that our best efforts are sometimes derailed by the unexpected exigencies of modern life.

If I have one regret it is that the words 'hurry' and 'quick' and 'now' seem to have echoed through my daughter's childhood as the drumbeat of her early years. Everything seems to be punctuated by the necessity of having to be or do according to the demands of the clock. If only we could all clock off from the cares and obligations of work and home and simply have the luxury of time to be the mother to the daughter. I know that I simply can't stretch time any further and that the elasticity of maternity can itself only stretch so far before it snaps. Time for a child is all afternoon in the park, looking at leaves and the shapes of clouds. Time for a mother is picking the older child up, doing the shopping, getting the dinner on, listening to the reading ... and running out of time.

Mothers check out each other's children and we are relieved when our youngsters are invited over to play. For every mother wants her child to be liked, to be included, to belong. They do not want fantastic results or odd behaviours or rejection. Just the sunny certainty of normality. And a mother's anguish over playground slights is never extinguished. For as Elizabeth Jolley says, 'A child is always the child of a mother' (*The Orchard Thieves*, 1995). The maternal heart still clutches with fear or opens with amazement no matter how old the child. In my late forties I am, still and always, my mother's daughter.

Other mothers tell me that Gracie is a kind child. I wish I could be a fly on the wall and see her as she is without my maternity intervening, commenting, insinuating itself visibly as it does when I am present. Because I know – as does every mother – that a child can be chameleon or changeling in their nature. I wonder what she is like away from me. I want to see her as others see her without the compulsions and obsessions that lay claim to her through me. I want to see her essence without the social dressing that I have imposed upon her. Be that as it may, I still want her to have that social dressing, the understandings and behaviours that will smooth her sailing into the vast waters of the world beyond the reaches of the parental pond. But ultimately, she will be her own person with our wishes and dreams and values and beliefs enmeshed quixotically in her uniqueness.

And she will, I hope, surprise us.

Over time she will learn that I am the best mum for her because I am the only one. She will come to understand that Mummy needs her own time scribbling, reading, singing, rekindling the woman she was; inventing the woman she might yet be. My daughter will not know that I have anguished briefly over my small dereliction of duty and that for me the intoxicating thrill spill of words has meant that she will be looked after by someone else for a few hours. But with that someone else there is *somewhere else — a somewhere else* experience that she can bring back to me at the end of the day. She can laugh and tell me about her day and I can listen in wonderment at the open book that childhood offers, each day an entry of new adventure and experience much of which she'll share with me, some of which I will never know.

And those things that I don't know and cannot reach are the private avenues of her own becoming. They are hers alone; to share if she wishes, to covet if that is her choice. I want her to have the space and time that allows her imagination to frolic, to sow the seeds of dream and destiny. And with my own time gathered greedily to my breast I plan to avoid the small harbours of resentment and regret, the weeds that sully memory and ambition. My daughter will not have to carry the burden of my life *manqué*.

The few hours I have wilfully spent in the corridors of creativity will add a spark to the me I need to be as mother, as wife, as sister, as daughter, as teacher, as human being. I will be girded by other interests and occupations when my daughter no longer needs me – quite as much. I will be busy in the other corners of my world. One day my daughter will say, 'My mother did that' and she will not berate me for the small incursion into the time we could have had together. Right now, as I type this up with two fingers, she talks to me about tomorrow's swimming lesson and what we will do on the weekend. Yesterday as she donned her glittery fairy wings to play boss fairy to her brood of Barbies, she asked me, 'When can I fly, Mummy?' and my heart turned over. A prayer that her wings would never be clipped sped skywards because in my mother's heart I know that the flight of dreams is a capricious one. An incantation of hope floats in the air.

Fly, darling, fly.

The birth of my daughter changed forever and immeasurably the contours of my life. My late motherhood has been a combination of the happy and the haphazard. I know that I am not all the things I could be for my daughter, but I am the one she comes to when she wakes up in the dark folds of night and needs my touch and murmuring to banish nameless fears that the nightlight can't dispel. My lullaby of love encircles her and she will wake, tomorrow and tomorrow, smiling and safe, to the invitation of a new day.

I am an imperfect mother.

But I'm giving the best of me – in whatever way it comes – to the little person who invited me into the mysterious and magical world of motherhood with its long hours, tears and smiles, small certitudes and large uncertainties. As most mothers of young children do, I am muddling along and managing. Just sometimes I need to remind myself of the person I was before the grace of childbirth rearranged my identity.

I am not defined or consumed by my motherhood, but it enhances much of who I am.

For that, I am blessed.

The youth of the nation are the trustees of posterity.

BENJAMIN DISRAELI

Edwina, I hope you have a blast in Byron Bay. I hope this first post-school celebration heralds a lifetime of chances and choices, some to do with career, some to do with love, but most to do with your own satisfaction, your own fulfillment. Yes, 'schoolies' is a rite of passage and a pat on the back for getting through those long years of secondary education, but it's also a bit of last hurrah as you dispense with some of your childish things and bowl headlong into the future. The shoreline of the known will disappear as you hike through the promontory of possibility. This will be the beginning of the adventure of your lifetime!

In the rococo bloom of middle age, and as one of those bloomin' baby boomers, my career trajectory (a loose definition for my hit-and-miss dabblings in various employments) has been more rollercoaster than A to B. I have stalled, stopped, taken scenic diversions, made ill-informed decisions, ignored good advice on the 'right direction' and done my own thing. But mainly I've followed my own internal compass and right now I'm where I want to be. That is not to say I'm now not going anywhere else, but the optimist in me likes to think that my options are still open, even if I am relatively settled in my current career.

My students, like you, are excited about life after Year 12. They are getting ready to stake their claim on the future, despite its unknowable quality. We talk about aspirations and ambitions and that the future is a nebulous thing. Just when we think we're there it changes shape or disappears or the goalposts are moved. The only constant is change and the youth of today have a career flexibility that is the envy of those still enslaved in the one job for life mentality.

Education is so much more than being trained to do a job. It is about giving students the confidence to take risks, taking chances on their own initiative, finding that inner motivation, perhaps doing those casual jobs that keep you fed while you're on the road to the next destination.

If anything, education should be about adaptability, about being able to manage new social situations, about being able to look beyond the mere exam result to the wider possibilities of all sorts of learning while traversing the road of life. It's about equipping our youth with the skills that enable them to 'have a go' at different enterprises, move out of the comfort zone of the known and the well-remunerated.

The stories I tell my students hinge on the adventures I had in my twenties and thirties. I tell of arriving penniless in the Channel Island of Guernsey. At least I had a job to go to and an attic room provided by my employer, but I did not know a soul. I reminisce about my days as 'Auntie Annie' in a Butlins-style holiday camp where I had to entertain bored kids from London housing estates. I tell tales of being a lounge singer, doing a jazzy spot for the sherry set on a Saturday night on the Isle of Man. And then, back to Melbourne after eight adventurous years, finally doing a Dip. Ed to become the teacher I was always destined to be.

Investments, Edwina, are for other people. I am investing in my life. I'm blessed with an easy-going husband and a whirlwind of a daughter. While my career might not hit the high spots of public recognition and acclaim, I know I'm doing some good in my small arena of influence. Invest in yourself and do what makes your heart sing. Worry about your HECS debt later.

This is your time so go ahead and make the memories that will keep you warm in later years. This is your turn. It is a time to break out with the thrills and spills that life will throw at you. However, this will not be the only time that you need to push out and challenge and stake a claim and party. When you have done something for many years, you may find the need to redefine who you are or be brave enough to tackle something new. It might be the time for surprises and reckonings and the full measure of accomplishments of various hues that comprise the story of a life. The break out of middle age has its compensations too. I admit I was a late bloomer, and I don't have the fiscal accoutrements of years in one career. I don't even suffer from status anxiety because, as I tell my friends in more glossy professions, teaching has become a second-tier profession, despite the fact that it is through the hearts and hands of these experts that the country is built. When you find what you love to do, do it, and do not listen to naysayers or those who insist that your income defines your success in the world.

As you will do, I have made my choices and from where I'm standing, they're pretty good. I'm still too young to worry about retirement villages and nursing homes. I'll leave that to other people's financial planners because I'm planning on having a good time.

So, have a great time, Edwina, in Byron Bay and create some happy memories as you undergo this rite of passage. Say thank you to the Red Frogs who keep an eye on all those who have partied a bit too hard. Leave your apartment relatively tidy. Ring home.

Put the career on the back burner for now. Enjoy

being young and free and forgive yourself the odd misstep as you start hiking towards the future. Find yourself and have fun and when you are my age, you'll be able to tell the tall tales and true stories of a life well lived.

Edwina, your time starts ... NOW!

This is an edited version of an article previously published in *The Sydney Morning Herald*, November 2015.

The fog comes on little cat feet ...

CARL SANDBERG

I'm on my rostered tram duty, in the fog during morning peak hour, on a main road in the leafy eastern suburbs. Decked out in my orange high-vis vest so the girls can avoid me as they tumble off the tram, I am at the lights to ensure they cross safely and get to school on time. There is a bit of dawdling, so I shoo them along knowing that the laughter and looking down at their phones means that they're in no particular hurry. It's only the bell that gets them moving at a more energetic pace.

My job is to check that they follow the road rules, wear the uniform properly and do a little meet and greet before they get to the front door. Some of the girls smile at me and say hello. The others seem to have forgotten that I taught them last year and am not invisible.

Buses have disgorged their passengers from the outer suburbs and a red-turbaned Sikh bus driver gives me a cheerful nod, a sort of complicit understanding that we are getting our charges to school safely. Trams emerge from the Deepdene dip like giant vehicular glow-worms. Trees are stiff spectral sentries in the grey soup of the unveiling morning. Noses pink and glisten. Under the tram shelter big boys stretch out of blazers. A lady smiles at me, perhaps acknowledging that this is just one of the myriad duties that are the teacher's lot. A couple of junior school girls *ooh* and *aah* over a fluffy dog being walked by its owner who is happy for them to pet it. A woman with green hair strides past purposefully and I admire her focus and fitness. A little girl in a puffer jacket escorts her three ginger-haired younger brothers, similarly attired, past the grey clump of girls gathered at the lights. I exchange thoughts about recent films with an affable film reviewing cleric who is off to an early screening at the Kino. A couple of corporate types shuffle impatiently, scrolling energetically on their smartphones. The traffic school is deserted, its tiny tram and train and scaled-down traffic lights yet to be occupied by kids on bikes learning the road rules that I am trying to enforce outside in the grown-up world. A Lycra-clad bike rider stops at the red light, his music blaring, perhaps afraid of being trampled by a great gaggle (or is that giggle?) of girls. Small children snug in car seats are buckled up. Older siblings gaze out smugly at those whose conveyance to school is public transport with its jam-packed camaraderie and occasional shows of courtesy for older passengers.

The lollipop man ensures the girls cross at the designated spot as a silver four-wheel drive gridlock threatens the equanimity of parents who are dropping off their precious cargo. The school's steeple and tower are shrouded in mist, looming out of the gloom like something from a Gothic horror novel. Any early morning eeriness is dispelled as soon as they saunter into the bright warmth of the entrance foyer.

It's a scene played out all across Melbourne; hordes of students travelling to school and dealing with the vagaries of the weather which doesn't seem to dim their youthful eagerness, even if they do have a Maths test after morning recess. As you drive past that person in a high-vis vest at tram, train or bus stops close to any school in the metropolis, think of the teacher as they complete yet another tour of duty.

It is the life of the crystal, the architect of the flake,
the fire of the frost, the soul of the sunbeam.
This crisp winter air is full of it.

JOHN BURROUGHS

We all experience winter differently, responding to these colder days according to our own dispositions and predilections. Some love the weather in its frosty flurries and rainy rantings, whilst others retreat to warmer climes to escape the chill sting of pins-and-needles hailstorms and slushy grey days. Geography, too, plays its role in the severity or mildness of this last of seasons, this wintry wayfarer, as it rolls and blusters and moans across the mountains, plains, coasts and deserts of this island continent.

For some, the cold seeps into bones to slow them down into lounging in front of a hibernating hearth to endure short days and long nights. This is mostly where I can be found, happy to harness the hours around me at the kitchen table where I jot and scribble and make impossible plans. Here, it becomes a time of gathering moon sung thoughts and pondering possibilities – where the dark muted hours offer solitude and rumination, gossamer reveries and evenings of books and fireside chat and the gentle mulling over of daylight things.

For others, it is the season that nips them into activity, prodding with its cold fingers to keep them energetic, to skate and ski and snowboard, to gather people together convivially, to play netball or football, to barrack passionately. My husband and I score at our daughter Gracie's netball game and watch as the girls' faces turn pink and pretty with the effort of keeping up with the speed and strategy of the game. Occasionally, they journey into the MCG to watch their beloved Richmond Tigers. Winter becomes the time when team colours warm the heart, worn as they are by those who have their allegiance tattooed into their psyche almost from birth. The team song becomes, especially after a win, a ruddy homecoming hymn.

Our Australian winters, depending on where we live, can be short and mild or long and lugubrious.

There can be days and weeks, even months, lashed with neon slits of lightning and furious fists of rain. There can be days of milky sunshine, surprise snow drops and the last tendrils of frost slipping off naked and shivering trees. There can be days of gutters gushing, leaping over puddles to get to work, leaping into puddles to get to school – days, too, of singing in the rain because of the joy of simply being alive to whatever the season throws at us.

However the winter weather is dispensed – arbitrarily, capriciously, a meteorological mayhem brewed in a cloudy cauldron with swells and floods and torrents and gale warnings and the inky innards of tempest – we have to live with it. We build winter into our days, recognising that it is a season with its own special consolations and an interiority denied us in brighter and longer hours. The weather may shape the day externally, deciding what jumper and raincoat we don, but it is the warmth of our hearts in winter that provides us with an internal barometer.

Albert Camus wrote, 'In the depths of winter I finally learned that within me there lay an invincible summer' (*Return to Tipasa*, 1952). Perhaps we can apply the metaphor of the seasons to our own lives. Some would say that winter harbours the end, that it is the last season of life before the new season of birth heralded by spring. But so much is going on unseen, underground, away from the bright disclosures of summertime when the living is easy. In this fallow time a new chapter is being written. The story is still being told. It's just that in winter the narrative thread becomes invisible because the world is denuded and leaves fall and birds hide and the days shorten so that dusk happens not long after school is out. This is winter's tale. But this is also a tale of resilience and regeneration, of subtle subterranean growth, of the burrowing in of survival, of battening-down and buttoning-up, of a primal story of seasons and crops and Mother Earth resting.

In literature, winter is often associated with old age, with time coming to an end, with a decrease in energy and imagination, a diminution of self. But in this winter of life there is much gathered wisdom. Australian painter John Olsen spoke of his renewed energy at 83. He asserted that he will, as Dylan Thomas' poem puts it, 'rage against the dying of the light' (*Do not go gentle into that good night*, 1951). It may well be the winter of his life, but this does not mean retiring or giving up or leaving all the fun to the youngsters. Instead, he is finding a winter wonderland, still enjoying childlike discoveries, being alert to grace notes and small wonders and tender mercies. He is alive to the songs and symphonies around him, perhaps heard differently or anew with the wisdom of his winter years. The colours of his life are as vibrant as ever.

The approach of the winter years compels us into an urgency to do something because time is running out. Passions and creativity are brought into sharper focus. Time is making, as Shakespeare put it, its thievish progress to eternity and we redouble our efforts. Perhaps we want to leave a mark, change careers or do some lasting good; some good that lives beyond us. Perhaps as time speeds up and we slow down we want our lives to resonate with the meaning we have spent a lifetime searching for.

William Blake wrote, 'In seed time learn, in harvest teach, in winter enjoy'. If we allow our lives to parallel the seasons, wintertime gathers up our experience, the jumbled joys and joustings, the wins and losses, the lessons learnt, and we impart the stories of hope and resilience and perseverance to those who come after us.

In winter we can fling our souls upon the gloom, as Thomas Hardy notes in his poem *The Darkling Thrush*. We can choose to resist the desolation that attempts to drag us into a quagmire of doubt and anguish. If we can live days full-hearted and joyous, nothing can stop the song being sung. I love the stoicism of my front yard sparrows that, despite the gloaming, still peek and putter along the branches. For me, those tiny, plumed aviators are heroic. Their winter hymn is one of cheerful solidarity, waiting out the winter weather together, side by side, soul to soul, keeping the cold out.

Most of us will experience a winter of the heart, not too distant from the dark night of the soul. This may be when a loved one has died and our mourning is deep, sometimes so deep that we feel we cannot go on, sometimes so deep that we go a little crazy. It may happen through abandonment or rejection or an accumulation of slights and sorrows. It is a time of emotional desolation – a winter of discontent. During this wintertime of the heart, it is wise to seek counsel and sometimes it is wise to take time to withdraw from the fray temporarily. At these times, our capacities have been dented and we need healing time. We are not at our best and it is no disgrace to admit it. We need to sideline ourselves. We need to wait for the propitious moment, the different psychic space or the dawning realisation that the worst is over.

The time will come again for new things.

As I enter the early autumn of my years and still feel the sun kiss of summer in my skin, I look back affectionately on the winters of my past. These were the primary school years of starched collars and grey gloves and neat little pinafores with Mother Flavia dispensing tomato soup for 5 cents from a giant pot in the school's concrete shelter shed. This is still the best soup I have ever tasted, leavened as it was by the love of a gruff elderly nun in her weathered wimple and black habit. Perhaps the taste has been enhanced by the blurred edges of happy memory where chubby fingered children recited prayers and times tables and the ballads of Banjo Paterson and C.J. Dennis's *The Triantiwontigongolope* and skipped and played chasey till the bell rang. I can still conjure up the smell of wet grey blazers, damp jumpers and moist mittens and the peculiar fug of travelling home on a crowded bus.

Winter was never an excuse for not doing anything.

We could still watch the bad-tempered clouds scud across the sky and wrap up warmly with nana-knitted scarves and stand too close to the three-bar radiator and play indoor chasey, the seven of us. And we loved the sudden discovery of rainbows as they stretched across the suburbs in a ribbon of colour, landing softly in the cleansed distance.

I still love rainbows after rain. They are nature's heraldic flags, marvellous decorative swags that bedizen the sky, a meteorological miracle that warms the winter heart.

If the sun and moon should ever doubt,
They'd immediately go out.

WILLIAM BLAKE

Fifty years ago, I sat in a cream-brick Melbourne school hall to see Neil Armstrong become the first man on the moon. His one small step for man and one giant leap for mankind opened up the heavens in a completely new way for an impressionable eleven-year-old. The moon and its mythology may have been conquered, but still I wished upon the stars. I had dutifully learnt the mnemonic 'My Very Elderly Mother Just Sat Upon New Paint' by heart in Grade 6 Science. Sadly, that tidy tiny full stop to the punctuation of planets, Pluto, was demoted to dwarf status in 2006. It may only be two-thirds the size of our moon, but it had sneaked into our affection as it resolutely kept to its elliptical orbit around the sun.

I was imbued with the happy acceptance that the moon kept an eye on earthly things. There may have been a man in the moon, but he was an avuncular old chap, protective and patient as he kept the tides to a timetable and eavesdropped on the sweet nothings of those who slipped home late under moonlight shadows. The moon was crescent or sliver, full or blue or blood. It created silhouettes and silverings. It was a button, a sixpence, a balloon, a gold doubloon, a saucer, an airless place of craters and mystery with its dark side permanently out of sight. Moonbeams, though, were anything but spectral. They were ribbons of light, subtle and mesmerising, glances and gleamings and glistenings that illuminated the swathe of time between dusk and dawn. In 1610, Galileo Galilei – that almost heretical helio-centrist to whom the Catholic Church has only recently apologised – wrote, 'It is a beautiful and delightful sight to behold the body of the moon.' And so, it is as our evenings bloom under this round and reliable heavenly body.

With the moon conquered the stars moved closer to me. They were shimmering sequins sewn into the dark velvet above. They offered me comfort as I stood in a back garden in Box Hill and surveyed the night sky. These stars were not dead or dying, nor mere light years away. They were part of the story of creation, beyond the rational science of the Big Bang, but a reason to believe in the divine, in God's hand on the wheel of eternity.

To think of the billions of stars in existence in a kaleidoscopic endlessness of space that cannot be measured or quantified is to know the miraculous. Genesis reminds us that God said, 'Let there be lights in the dome of the sky to separate the day from night; and let them be for signs and for seasons and for days and years, and let them be lights in the dome of the sky to give light upon the earth.' And so, we have the greater light, the sun, and the lesser light, the moon. They have marked the passage of each day's journey since the beginning of time.

In winter in Melbourne the six o'clock news glows greyly into lounge rooms across the city while the stars blink above unseen. The moon has brimmed the horizon and is stationed in its usual spot, loitering luminously, watching that all is as it should be. The crystal clarity of the night sky is blurred by suburban street lighting although I can still pick out the Southern Cross and the Saucepan. Sometimes, through the haze on a sharp shivery night, I see a star glisten in ice-blue incandescence. In the country the velvet ether is unassailed. Scintillas of starlight dapple the night sky, cosmic confetti that lifts the heart. I am humbled and exalted as I gaze at the tent of heaven above.

D.H. Lawrence wrote, 'Be quite alone and feel the

living cosmos softly rocking' (*The Complete Poems*, 1957). I may be alone with my thoughts when I glance covetously at the moon, but I am connected to every person who has ever gazed upwards and wondered about their place in the schemes of things; in God's plans for us, as individuals and as the human race. They are ponderings existential and domestic, profound and passing, eternal and ephemeral. The moon glows – and listens to our confessions and confidences. Beneath her shimmer, I am enveloped in gratitude and wonder. I stand with Cleopatra and Hildegard of Bingen and Joan of Arc and Queen Victoria, princesses and peasants, saints and sinners, the high and low born of every generation; all the women who have come before me; all who have sighed under the moon and basked in her benevolent democracy.

I look above and imagine the hand of God in sweeping strokes, in novas and galaxies, in black holes and dwarf planets and comets and constellations and in the moon's Sea of Tranquillity. I imagine the stories of the stars, the Magi following the star to Bethlehem, the stars guiding mariners and adventurers beyond the flat earth to the new world, the stars that twinkle for children as they look to the sky and realise we are not alone. I look at the moon and find it a friendly presence, a giant nightlight that dispels ghosts and ghouls in dark corners and glows with unflinching constancy. Hers is a tender voyeurism – the night-watch of love. She is not Noyes' 'ghostly galleon tossed upon cloudy seas' of the poetry learnt by rote in a beige classroom adjacent to that hall where we were shuffled in to watch the grainy footage of history a lifetime ago. She is steadfast as she waxes and wanes and keeps to her ancient course.

During these quiet brittle hours our moon is the homecoming queen of the night. She does not worry that the distant stars might be brighter and more thrilling. She is unconcerned that the Milky Way spirals and scintillates in vast galaxies beyond our solar system. She has her own measure. She pales in the bright light of big brother, Sun, but hangs happily in her own kindly light; little sister Moon with her fairy-dust motes and tinsel beams, her complicity and mystery and memory.

She has a vigilante soul.

She is night's heroine; mistress of the tides, companion of the clouds, the dream weaver of the small hours, that grand theatrical dame of dance and song and poetry beloved by the captive audience of our own blue planet.

She is the lamplight on the corner of a familiar street for old Mother Earth.

This is an edited version of an article previously published in *Melbourne Catholic*, July 2019.

The props of life ... titles, uniforms, rank, cars, house, social circles ... are only that; the little marks we use to let people know how important we are. It's what we are without them that really matters.

SAINT THÉRÈSE OF LISIEUX

The sturdy backpack containing lunch, a half-read novel and some corrected homework is humped onto my spine. It's an ungainly lump, but the daily trek to work is about practicality, not fashion sensibility. After a minute or two I begin to stride into a rhythm, a buoyant stepping out into the promise of a new day, the uplifting prayer of the possible. It's a day that has never been before or will be again and I have my very own walk-on role.

As the world shakes off its slumber and clouds curl into the blue beyond I begin to frame my day, to put a shape around it. I do this by having a quiet word with God as I hit the road. It might even look a bit like I am talking to myself, but that's fine as these days it seems everybody's talking volubly as they walk around city streets and invite strangers to eavesdrop on the minutiae of their lives. My words fly up accompanied by the bump and grind of peak hour traffic, a low vehicular hum heading towards the CBD. I maintain a steady pace, not quite a soft shoe shuffle, but a purposeful perambulation to journey's end – school. I offer him my thoughts, stop-start, alert not alarmed efforts, as I keep an eye on cars backing out, the pedalling paper boy, the serious runners, the busy intersection ... the others who walk on by. I pass shuttered shops with sleeping mannequins dreaming of being real. Hardy hydrangeas nod as I puff past and newspapers play dead on footpaths.

My greetings to God are composed of loosely connected fragments, small scintillas of thought, strung together with the glue of gratitude. They do not have the formal elegance or meditative quality that would flower in the calm cocoon of the chapel. They are practical work-a-day, walk-a-day prayers for the urban pilgrim, prayers for the busy road, not the leafy avenue. I am glad God speaks all languages because my prayers could so easily be lost in translation. He makes sense of what I am trying to say, the giddy grammar and poor punctuation. And much as they are prayers, they are also the thinkings-out for the day ahead and the occasional necessary rehearsal or practice of words that might need to be said or issues made known.

As I unburden myself my backpack doesn't seem quite so heavy. I am lightened.

Pedestrian prayers.

Or prayers for pedestrians.

It's what you read when you don't have to that determines what you will be when you can't help it.

OSCAR WILDE

Books, as artefacts or objects, tell tales about their owners. The disordered piles on a desk, the teetering spire next to the bed, the bulging bookcase in the study, the artfully placed coffee table book or the priceless first edition lend a certain aesthetic to any room. But with the rise of e-readers and the imminent digitisation of the world's libraries, will the delights of the home library become a thing of the past? Local schools are closing libraries to cater for future learning, but I wonder about the future of learning if our students do not read beyond their digital devices, if they are not exposed to ideas and imaginations beyond the bubble of algorithmic confirmation bias, the glitterati and the Twitterati.

Books open up the world. They extend our knowledge, expand our imaginations and create empathy for people and situations beyond the comfort and safety of our own lives. Books can provoke, challenge and disturb and they can rhapsodise, venerate and affirm. In an age of instant gratification and sensory overload, the printed book can slow us into calmer rhythms and a more thoughtful process of accession. For me, the gift of reading is incalculable.

I have been accused of wasting time reading. Wasting time! How can it be wasting time when a writer's efforts are changing my world, enlightening me, making me joyful, making me think bigger and brighter, making me dream in celestial colours, not pegging me down to the small and drear and disappointed? My dear long-suffering husband knows that if I am reading it is fairly likely that dinner will be pretty last minute, something with Chicken Tonight, and that the evening meal is merely an interruption to time spent luxuriating in the world of words. He knows that I am a wordy woman and he wouldn't have me any other way, except when I have the last word in our robust discussions about literary merits and missteps.

I like bookcases that look as though human hands have recently riffled through a thesaurus or reread a favourite short story. I like bookcases where a book of poetry, say, Bruce Dawe's *Sometimes Gladness* is on snuggling terms with old school annuals, the signed first novel of a friend, *Of Mice and Men* and some well-thumbed Penguin paperbacks; the books that have burrowed into your psyche, the books that you take with you every time you move, bound friends.

Salman Rushdie says that we read our lives through books; that in some strange alchemy they become part of us; that they help name our world. Right now, I am reading Anne Tyler's *Back When We Were Grown Ups* and in her words and story I find myself going back and wondering what became of me, just as her main character does. The joy of reading allows me to dwell and ruminate and wonder; to curl up and into myself and be transported. This joy is so profound that I want to pay homage to that strange lyric compulsion; to write what I can as well as I can; to bow before the writers who inspire me and borrow egregiously to smarten up my own efforts, to infuse the pedestrian with a little poetry, to give my words wings.

I wonder what my bookcase says about me and my world. It probably confirms this interest in writing with its reference books and dictionaries and a handy compilation of Oscar Wilde's most pithy epigrams. It makes plain that I don't read science fiction or fantasy and that crime fiction, much as I enjoy some of it, is not given shelf space except, of course, for Agatha Christie's genre-extending *The Murder of Roger Ackroyd*. At the moment I only have one autobiography, Brenda Niall's *Still Life*, bought because she was at school with my mother. I have a couple of Austens and a few Dickens and a recent Booker winner, *The Gathering* – a story about a big family which will be passed on to one of my six siblings. I have my mother's Palgrave's *Golden Treasury* and a book of poems by Rupert Brooke that my father gave her when they first married. A tatty Norton's *Anthology of Poetry* is a reminder of happily misspent days on the lawn outside the Baillieu Library. I have books on spirituality and poetry and a couple of travel books reminding me of places in my heart. My sister bought me Patti Smith's *Devotion* while we travelled through Harrisburg, Pennsylvania and I bought myself *The Guernsey Literary and Potato Peel Pie Society*, long before it was dreamed into the film, because I spent eighteen happy months on that Channel Island thirty years ago.

I have bought books from bargain bins and at markets and op shops, at well-known bookstores, deceased estate auctions, school fetes, country antique bazaars, specialist bookshops, The Merchant of Fairness and at Dirt Cheap Books whose enviro bag I quickly offloaded because of its conspicuous lack of cachet. I have borrowed and placed books at the tiny Little Library in Melbourne Central and have happily sat there browsing and wondering about the other odd bods who are peeking and picking from the shelves.

I love knowing other people have read books before me, especially when I see inscriptions or comments or doodles or I find old bookmarks or tram tickets that have marked the page years before. Sometimes reviews are tucked inside the book, the critic's reading lending authority to the original purchase. I have also noticed that readers are an assiduous lot who are keen to correct editing and typographical mistakes that have somehow not been picked up prior to publication. Incorrect spelling or typos are circled emphatically. I am guilty of this too! Why, only yesterday I was reading a Minette Walters murder mystery, *The Shape of Snakes*, and noticed 'sight' instead of 'sigh' on page 56. A recent reading of David Malouf's moving short stories in *Dream Stuff* had a previous reader savagely score out an errant 'h' in 'selves' which had somehow becomes 'shelves'.

I often bang on about proofreading to my students who have now developed the habit of alerting me to mistakes in all sorts of public spaces: signage, news reports, the newspaper, the school text books we are studying. Yay! They may be the next generation who will care that things are done properly and well and that the written word is in safe hands.

And then, of course, there is the marginalia which adds another layer of intrigue to the reading experience. The act of reading can be so immersive that sometimes the reader has to respond jubilantly to beautiful words or critically if they feel that an idea is muddied by self-indulgent verbiage. Charles Kingsley wrote he knew the topography of each book's blots and dog ears and could trace the dirt in it to having read it with tea and buttered muffins. My bequest to those who read after me will be tiny flecks of roast almond dark chocolate.

On the Australian front I have a Garner and a Stead, and Lawson's short stories, and my Year 12 copy of *The Getting of Wisdom*. Eliot Perlman's *Three Dollars* is a recent favourite and Clive James' rambunctious freewheeling memoirs strike a chord. I have recently enjoyed *The Dry* by Jane Harper, cleverly using the school library to curb the efflorescence at home. Camus and Dostoevsky may have resided on the bookshelves of my past, but the past is another country. I was a different reader then and sometimes even classics outlive their shelf life. And I am happy to read unfashionably; to find enjoyment in out-of-print books and the good reads of yesteryear. I love J.B. Priestley.

My bookcase is dominated by fiction and is absolutely lacking in sociological, business or political reads. I will not house celebrity pulp or anything that suggests I can improve my life, finances or career prospects. No new age, or how-tos and no, no, no cookbooks. Thin collections flirt with fat omnibuses. They lean lopsidedly against John Banville's *The Sea*, a book I can only describe as swimming in silk, so gorgeous is the prose that sometimes I have to simply stop reading to savour the felicity of his chosen words and ponder his obsession with the word flocculent. And I am not above a bit of up lit – *Eleanor Oliphant is Completely Fine* is absolutely fine.

Jorge Luis Borges believed that paradise would be a kind of library. So where does this leave the humble bookcase, once the feature of the family room, before the plasma took centre stage? Will there no longer be homes for dog-eared, well-thumbed, revisited old favourites that can be put down and picked up with a sigh of contentment and the heart's ease of a good read? Will visitors no longer serendipitously pick up a book because it looks interesting or has a great opening line or is a hallowed work and ask to borrow it? Will books become curiosities, lumpen artefacts, tomes to be toted to Vinnies as we robotically turn to the TV or our devices to watch the film version and are anaesthetised into torpor by Netflix and its easy addiction?

My bookcase, crammed with books of all shapes and sizes, of great and sometimes questionable quality, of authors renowned and authors obscure, some a little tired and tattered because of frequent reference and continued delight, will continue to furnish my room. I am in happy agreement with Pulitzer Prize winner Anna Quindlen who wrote, 'I would be most content if my children grew up to be the kind of people who think decorating consists mostly of building enough bookshelves' (*The New York Times*, August 1991).

My library was dukedom large enough.

WILLIAM SHAKESPEARE

It's a mid-November morning on one of those can't-make-up-its-mind Melbourne days. First grey, then glimmery with weak sunshine, then spackled with fugitive raindrops, then woolly warmish grey again. I'm at the State Library to do some research; to sit under the Dome as others have done before me – and others will do after me – and to make sense of an historical slice of time and some key events in it. I'm working on a family story about art and adventure and need certain facts and dates to peg down my imaginative flights of fictional fancy. I've walked past the statues of Saint George and the Dragon and Saint Joan of

Arc on guard outside this august building and into its grand columned portico. Past the friendly security guards, I begin to feel the rich hum of democracy that pervades this heralded institution and its open-door policy to all who enter.

I walk in to see Victor Hugo's words emblazoned on the walls: 'Words are the mysterious visitors of the soul.' As I sit and wrestle with words and their mystery, I am thankful that I can do this in such conducive surroundings; a preternatural hush is still the code of conduct in the La Trobe Reading Room. There is a certain civility of demeanour in those who gather here in solitary joy or student cluster or tourist appreciation. In 1854, the library was declared to be open to everyone over the age of fourteen, 'even though he be coatless ... if only his hands are clean'. I like to think my hands are always clean as I jot and type and look around me and wonder about words and paragraphs and synonyms and if anyone will ever read my middle-brow efforts.

Between waiting for the elusive muse and riffling through reference books, I look up to see a girl I taught fifteen years ago leaning against a balcony pillar. She is now a beautiful woman. In her white wedding dress, she and her husband pose patiently for the photos they may one day show their grandchildren, who could well be amused at the *olden* days of 2015.

Outside, in the forecourt, the world passes by. Five young men kneel and pray as they create a sacred space in the midst of the midday throng. An older man wearing a beret and with a white rose in his lapel stops to watch two young men as they play chess with pieces the size of toddlers. Interested onlookers gather briefly and a pair of backpackers snag a seat. A middle-aged couple kiss, friends meet and greet and men in suits stride purposefully to their lunchtime meetings. A school group squawks excitedly and a seagull perches proprietorially on the head of Joan of Arc who gazes imperturbably into the Swanston Street crowd.

About two years ago I was approached to do an impromptu video about people who frequented the library – just the odd bods who burrow down into the books and seem at home. Perhaps it was because I was sitting on the floor with an array of art reference books around me looking for information on Max Meldrum and his school and was dressed in talk-to-me bright red. I was asked to say something about an event/idea/person that mattered to me, so I began talking – in my best English teacher voice – about Joan of Arc and the discovery I had made in a small parish church in the middle of France. In a village called Parassy, which comprised a *tabac*, a petrol station and perhaps twenty or thirty houses, the somewhat neglected parish church, adjacent to the small town square, contained a lovely stained-glass window of Joan as a peasant girl praying. This was long before all the voices and the military leadership and her reinvention as the Maid of Orleans. This was just a young girl with a life ahead of her; a girl captured in that innocence before new ideas and other visions reshape the character that has been formed in the family. I spoke about the person we are as teenagers and how life has other plans for us and how we so rarely see Joan without her armour. And it reminded me of the quote that I had stumbled across about faith being a fragrance and not a suit of armour; something to be worn lightly, illuminatingly, without the dark division of doctrine and dogma.

I'd forgotten about this interview until almost a year later when one of my Year 12s told me she had seen me on the big screen at the State Library as she did some cramming for mid-year exams. I was thrilled to be on YouTube and insisted all my Year 7s watch it as a bit of a History/RE lesson combo. My likes tally amounted to the grand sum of about thirty.

Inside on the ground floor students share exam tips and cram nervously and solitary readers are oblivious to everything but the words on the page or device in front of them. Smooth young Law students tutor by the hour helping VCE students understand the intricacies of the text response. Researchers delve into old newspapers and retirees trace their family story. At my large, shared desk, I wonder about the words being written and typed here. Novels, theses, words of comfort, research papers, love letters, lists, travelogues, prayers; the sorting and sifting of words into purpose and meaning. I am editing these words, trying to work out some sort of coherent theme for a proposed work, trying to get my words to work in a way that the imagined reader will like. I admit to being something of a literary vagrant with my piecemeal efforts, but I still get a thrill when I finally see something published. And as with many of my trying writer friends, we feel proper validation is print publication and being paid for it and not the call for any sort of content filler that cheapens the effort of those who care about words in a way that is more than advertorial or adversarial. Still, I know in my heart that it is the day job of teaching that enables me to play with words on the weekend, so here I am again happily ensconced under the bright natural light of the grand Victorian dome.

The little green table lamp shines benignly as I sit in my usual seat near the books on Australian politics. I arrived here at 10 o'clock to secure my seat but had a quick look at the shelves and found a book on Barry Humphries called *Flashbacks* which detailed his theatrical career. This was fatal and there was my first hour gone. And I do plan to have a tuna, egg and cos lettuce baguette at Mr Tulk on the way out and perhaps poke my head into Readings to see what the latest offerings are. Such is the aspiring writer's life!

I have availed myself of the call-up system for obscure books burrowed deep into the library; a small monograph by the eight-time Archibald winner William Dargie written in 1957 that may not see the light of day again, unless someone writes his autobiography. The system is remarkably efficient. I've managed to chase up some paperwork relating to an arts festival held almost seventy years ago. I've sat in the newspaper section going through old papers and have comfortably taken up carpet space in the art reference area when no seats were available. In fact, people seem to sit, crouch, lean and make themselves comfortable with their laptops in all sorts of nooks and crannies. It draws people of all ages and inclinations into a place that refuses no-one, whether they want to use a computer or a microfiche or browse the new releases or meet a group of friends or just sit for a while with their nose in a book.

One of the big drawcards at the State Library of Victoria is Ned Kelly's armour and I, too, wander along to see it, thinking about that last stand at Glenrowan and the man in the iron mask. I read all the material about him and see the Jerilderie Letter and think about the grievances he may have had. His death mask is not scary. (I note that there is no mention of young Ned's bravery as an eleven-year-old in saving Richard Shelton from drowning in Hughes Creek at Avenel, for which he was awarded the green sash he wore at the fateful shoot-out. I admit my partiality here because my sister, Dominique, nursed till his death the last of Richard's children, Britton Shelton, who grew up knowing that Ned Kelly was a local larrikin lad who had pluckily saved his father's life.) Ned's armour is the focal point of the exhibition The Changing Face of Victoria, which is a fascinating story of Victoria's history with artefacts, photos, logbooks, diaries, lithographs and political cartoons all curated in a way that is accessible and interesting to either the avid history buff or the meandering school student.

On the sixth floor I gaze down into the Dome Room from a vantage point next to the Shakespeare Window with its nod to 'all the world's a stage'. The Mirror of the World exhibition on the fifth floor tells the story of the printed book and the collection ranges from the illustrated manuscript *Scriptores Historiae Augustae* (1492) made for Lorenzo de' Medici to the beautiful botanical illustrations of the eighteenth century and the pulp fiction of the 1950s. For those who love books as physical entities, it is a treat and a reminder that in this digital age eBooks can never furnish a room the way loved books do.

The State Library of Victoria is a glorious building and under its Dome I join a writing fraternity of past, present and future. It is where words inhabit the very ether and minds take flight under its warm cascading light. It has been called a cathedral of space. It is a place for the words of the soul and a welcome to all who browse and borrow, sit and think, wonder and write.

And for me, well, heaven would have to be a library.

In the beginning was the Word, and the Word was with God, and the Word was God.

JOHN 1:1

The Melbourne Writers Festival is a huge, wordy, whimsical, wise, witty, winter gathering of those who live and breathe words. These words are not solely the words in books, but words in blogs and forums, in tweets and podcasts, in zines and journals, in public performance and private viewing; words streaming to us from all over the globe. They are words read quietly or words performed to noisy crowds. They are words reshaped and recreated to reach and touch us; sometimes they soothe, sometimes they shake us up; sometimes they are scintillating, sometimes they are scathing.

How we use the words in our lives says much about who we are.

No matter the platform, we internalise words because they so often provide us with intellectual, emotional or spiritual sustenance. They nourish us at the deepest level. We also acknowledge that there are words that can demonise and appal, words that sow war and wounds, words that should not become part of private or public discourse because they lessen who we are. We need to be discerning and civil in the words we speak or write or forward on or like. As the Persian poet Hafiz said, 'The words you speak become the house you live in.' The words we speak and the words we listen to inform who we are; they can enlighten or eviscerate, deify or denigrate.

I am a woman of my words.

We read for a variety of reasons: for diversion, enlightenment, fun, to open our minds to other people and places and to expand our thinking. We read to stretch ourselves beyond our bias and worldview, to probe ambiguities and doubts. Many of us read to become better people; we allow others' words to infiltrate so that we can venture beyond our own bubble of ease and complacency. Sometimes we need to be prodded and provoked, moved beyond postcode insularity to new attitudes and consequent actions.

Sometimes we just want the blessing of beautiful

words to gift us with a new and rarefied understanding. If we are lucky, we find the writer or wordsmith who speaks our language. And sometimes, all we want is the beach read, the soporific text that doesn't demand too much of us, something pleasantly forgettable. We don't always have to do improving reading.

There are times and places and moods for the different weights of words.

In the waters of the womb we hear the soothing words of existence. At the breast we are suckled to the swoon of the lullaby. As we learn to read and write, the wonder of our own capacity to use words excites us. At school we work at words, getting them wrong, kneading them into shape, stretching our vocabularies, experimenting with structure and shape and sound, learning to use them in proper sentences. Then come the essays and words are invested with a new power because they can argue, make a point, stand up for themselves, stand for what you stand for. We discover that words can be good and bad. They can rage or rhapsodise, venerate or violate, exhort or excoriate. They can be used with love or hate.

We celebrate the giftedness of writers; the poets and philosophers from high academe, the backblock bards, suburban sages, hipster hellraisers. Each, in their own way, contribute to the life of the mind, for in their offerings, we move beyond that small frame of reference – ourselves. Every time we read, we are immersed in other furrows of thought and we temporarily cease our own self-involvement. We are liberated from the tedium of self and that same-old story. We know that we have great and minor word artists, middling and marvellous workers for the word, and that we eventually find our own level; the words that work for us. For some, it is highly cerebral stuff which takes time to understand and internalise. For others, it might be populist and easily digestible. We do not always have to work hard with words to make them sparkle for us.

In the ancient words of our sacred texts we come to realise who we are. Over the years those words bring us home, their familiar repetition a humming in the soul; grace notes that bind us to the tradition into which we were born. These texts set out the wisdom and teaching of each faith in words that believers etch into their collective memory. In the credos and the creation stories, the paths or the ways to enlightenment, each tradition uses words as touchstones for the spirit. In these texts there are parables and poetry, psalms and proverbs, words that have spoken to the human condition for thousands of years; words that have comforted and counselled; words that have inspired and instructed; words of joy and justice and judgement. As Proverbs 16:24 reminds us, 'Gracious words are like honeycomb, sweetness to the soul and health to the body.'

Often we forget to acknowledge the God-given talent that enables words to work their magic. For it is in the integrity of those words, in their wonder and revelation – and occasional prophetic caution – that we find solace and hope. Those words, brewed through time, temperament and creative hard work, can wreak changes in the heart and mind; they can change lives. Some writers peer into our souls and ask that we do better. They place a mirror to our lives and expose the cracks. Fiction or fact, they can confront us with the good and bad, the banal and the brutish. In the unique welter of their words, they tell it how it is. Some writers can bring us closer to God in the beauty and sensitivity of their insights. They can articulate our thoughts when we are dumbstruck. They can write a truth in such a way that we see it for the first time. And, sometimes, that truth is a blunt instrument because it needs to be.

Words can ennoble when they find the places in the heart. They tune the soul to goodness, truth and beauty – or a harsh and unjust reality. Sometimes, they tune the mind to a rollicking good read or the soft sibilance of poetry or the minutiae of a great life. On occasion, an escape into words is all we need to reinvigorate ourselves for the busyness beyond the page. Words have wings. They have the power to transport us to other times and places, to see our better selves in heroes, to beckon us to new worlds of understanding, to find common ground, to humanise us. American writer Wallace Stevens reminds us that 'the word is the making of the world'.

In a world that is word-weary because words have

become wounds and weapons, we need to think about how our own words, in our real and digital lives, are making the world around us.

The right words are balm for wounds, vision in the fog of venality, springboards for action, words with which to fly. The right words right the world. As we continue to talk and write and email and text and read and communicate with each other, we must use our words wisely. Uttered, they cannot be unsaid. Written, they cannot be deleted. We need to build that vocabulary of affirmation and agency that touches the angel of our better selves. Our words must be generous and inclusive, words that consult and invite and acknowledge.

Words have heart and heft, weight and wonder, power and prescience and presence.

We need to honour what we say, how and when and where.

How wonderful it would be if we could all be taken at our (best) words.

This is an edited version of an article previously published in *Melbourne Catholic*, August 2019.

*None are so old as those
who have outlived enthusiasm.*

HENRY DAVID THOREAU

Instead of discovering on the further side of fifty that I am stuck in a twilight zone that defines and confines my ambition and the longevity of my dreams, I have now been delivered some seriously good news. I am, thanks to the futurists who badge and reconstitute social demographics into ever more refined descriptions, a potentialist. That I may be working, in some form or another, until I am seventy, rather than being retired, is an opportunity for reinvention and discovery. I probably won't be a lady who lunches, but

I'll volunteer, provide elder wisdom to young people, follow my passions and be grateful for every single day. I'll be getting on with my life list, which I think is a much more hopeful term than bucket list.

Apparently, potentialists are those whose life experience and career trajectories have led them to a certain place and time where they now want to explore their lived potential. Perhaps they have seen the warning signs of redundancy or retirement or the swim-between-the-flags limitations of part-time work or the long years without the structure and sociability of getting up and going to a job. Perhaps they are putting in the last few years to shore up a future upon which they have particular designs. After years of indentured tenure or wage slavery or increased casualisation, the subjugation of the creative gene to the exigencies of survival, mortgages and school fees, the bureaucratic capriciousness of middle management on the treadmill of time and talent wasted, potentialists have dreams they want to achieve … yesterday.

We may never have been the next big thing, the best and the brightest, someone to watch as we drove a stake into the future and marked out our real or digital fiefdom. We may have been mere foot soldiers in the workforce, the humdrum worker bees, whose kaleidoscopic dreams of youth were diverted by other urgencies. Perhaps we were not brave enough. Perhaps we were not lucky or entrepreneurial or networked prodigiously or namedropped shamelessly. Perhaps we lacked the chutzpah or believed in the old-fashioned virtues of humility and loyalty and understood that big noting oneself was a taboo. Perhaps we weren't driven enough, gently treading water in our known securities, not quite ready to break the mould, living someone else's life and waiting for ours to begin.

Not anymore. With an ageing population, potentialists are the next big thing. They are not going anywhere quietly or demurely. They are ready to seize the day. They are not waiting for permission. Potentialists have a youthful mindset and the age and experience to go with it. They are past the age of having to impress others. They do not have to bend over backwards to please the boss or work unreasonably long hours. They do not have to spend more time at the office, writing reports for their immediate superior, reports that will be shredded within six months when the latest fad takes hold and the staff has to be retrained in a new lexicon and brand-speak.

Potentialists are finally finding out who they are and what they want to do, even if it has taken almost two thirds of a lifetime. They have done the hard yards with work and family and now it's their turn. Some may still be working because they need to or want to. Some may like the sense of connection that the workplace offers. Some may be thinking about tree or sea changing. Some may be changing down a gear; some may be revving up because they realise that time is on the wing. And the potentialist typology offers so much more colour and excitement than the less-than-inspirational descriptor 'grey nomad' which, it seems to me, carries a slightly spectral shadow.

For many of us, the real moment of success is not the one that others necessarily notice. Sometimes it is the slow burn of years of effort that suddenly blazes into public awareness. It is the quiet satisfaction that comes with late blooming. Sometimes success truly takes a lifetime.

For potentialists, the future is a fabulous second lease of life. We are getting ready to come out and play. The encore career awaits!

*I like the Gown very much &
my Mother thinks it very ugly.*

JANE AUSTEN

Back in the early 1960s my mother would load the five under ten of us into her Hillman, affectionately known as GUK because of its numberplate, and we would squabble from Kew to Swan Street in the sibling skirmishes of any sort of car travel. She would curb crawl to find a park that didn't necessitate a long walk with the four girls and the one boy none too keen to be attached to this petticoat pilgrimage.

She taught us the joys of shopping well. She may have had an account at Georges with the ladies-who-lunched-set, but she knew the value of shopping around and how to layer her looks, seasoning high-end labels with something less expensive. She took pride in being able to turn us out fashionably without totally depleting her housekeeping. My father marvelled at her ability to spend so wisely and well. Later, when we were all off to school, my mother would become one of the original clothing recyclers at Camberwell Market on a Sunday morning. She established tasteful little outlets in Ivanhoe and Kew where women of her ilk came to buy and borrow and laugh a little at their own fashion foibles. For my mother, fashion was always about fun and she never needed to dress to impress.

Dimmeys, with its famous green globe and clock tower, had come to epitomise Richmond as much as Punt Road, St Ignatius, and the Bourke, Barrot and Clay centreline of the Tigers in their glory days. Shoppers of all persuasions and incomes enjoyed the retail therapy of rag trade samples, bottom of the bin bargains, unusual best buys and the magical miscellany that this erstwhile emporium offered its clientele over the years.

The writing was on the wall years before it eventually closed. With a basket full of odds and ends I trundled over to order a cappuccino at the Goodness Gracious café – next to the Berlei bras and the job lot of the previous summer's T-shirts at $5.99 each. I was shocked to see the sign: 'Closed – thank you for your patronage'. No more sitting on a rickety bentwood chair and idly perusing old copies of *New Idea*. No more looking at the photos pinned to the wall or the sales sheets of the early twentieth century when Dimmeys was Dimelows – manufacturers and importers – and the currency was sterling and the women wore long frocks to go shopping. No more $2.50 for a cheese and tomato toastie and a coffee with a slice of life to go.

After rummaging through menswear for my husband and sampling testers in the cosmetics section I'd head to this small corner of sanity in the sales rush. I'd watch clutches of grandmothers, blue-rinsed and buoyant, clucking over children; teenagers riffling through the racks to find something decent on their babysitting budget. Young mums would sag into the seats as their progeny in pushers begged for a 20-cent jam fancy from the glass jar on the counter. The single gerbera on the table added a touch of homeliness. Occasionally a beautiful woman, resplendent in high fashion, would pop into the store for a quick tour after having reconnoitred the posher outlets up on Bridge Road.

Over the years I have lay-byed manchester and towels and Christmas presents and have always been happy with the no-nonsense service that packed purchases into the big red bag and sticky-taped it together. I still have a pair of beautiful vases hidden high in the kitchen cupboards, bought on impulse twenty years ago, and waiting for the right house in which to be displayed. Those black Lipstik shoes I snaffled some years ago are back in fashion. A pair of pendulous blue earrings add a touch of the exotic to my work-a-day attire.

My daughter's first haircut was at Dimmeys seventeen years ago where we waited till our ticket number was called. Here her bad hair day was transformed with a quick snip and a red lolly. And through all those years the refrain 'Mr Camparesi to the register' was a backing track to my shopping adventures as I traipsed through untidy aisles and perused the flyers with their marvellously normal models with life-size busts and buttocks wearing nighties and no-name leisure wear. These were not glossy girlies with the sleek shine of haute couture, but real people wearing real clothes. No airbrushed gimmickry or brand power, no florid copy or stratospheric prices. No supermodels with their oh-so-minute naked imperfections, just real women whose catwalk was the kitchen or the office or the factory floor. Off my feet I could sit down and make lists, do my own mental stocktake, catch my breath and treat my daughter to a giant sausage roll with sauce which she would eat with gusto.

Dimmeys catered to a populace on a budget who could mix and match it. It was a store that spelt spillover, rummage and finally finding that oddment that completed the set. It was about job lots and end of lines and strange assortments and clearance sales and massive markdowns and tat and trinketry. Such was my dismay at the closure of the café that I rang the store to register my protest. One of the small predictable pleasures in my life had been erased. Management told me that the café wasn't cost effective. Another loss to the insatiable imperative of profit.

When I explore Swan Street, I don't want to sit in a groovy juice bar. I want to sit in a place that affords me good coffee while I observe the *passeggiata* of families shopping and dropping. On my goodbye visit a couple of years ago, I resisted buying the grey singing steering wheel cover playing *Hot Stuff* at $3.99. I did buy a book about Elvis for my brother, a sturdy baking tray and some flannelette pyjamas that are just the job for winter.

The grand old dame Dimmeys is gone – replaced by slick apartments that old Richmond families can no longer afford. Still, I learnt from my mother that great lesson of delayed gratification where saving for something and paying it off via lay-by meant that I experienced the joy of anticipation, even if it was only for some rather flouncy bedding. These days, shopping is all about the experience, but I still fondly remember the foraging and finding of things that no other store would dream of selling. It wasn't designer or hip, and its displays didn't have clean lines or any sort of merchandising edginess, but it was a place where you could bag a bargain. It's where I learnt to shop well and to know when I was being hoodwinked by high street stores and their come-hither labels. Perhaps I am showing my age and my retail predilections, but Dimmeys in Swan Street will always have a soft spot in this shopper's heart.

*Beauty is not in the face;
beauty is a light in the heart.*

KAHLIL GIBRAN

Once again, no invitations to launches or wrap parties or VIP shopping extravaganzas. No exclusive gatherings worshipping at the feet of wafer thin, Bambi-eyed beauties. No reserved seating by the runway or a post-show party for the best dressed. It seems Melbourne Fashion Festival has overlooked me ... again. If I'm lucky I might just grab it by its disappearing coattail at Chaddy.

For this 16+, 50+, ample-hipped, small-statured, well-endowed suburban goddess, fashion means having something clean to wear to work. Higgledy hems and straining seams are artfully covered with scarves and brooches. Earrings distract from the more garish misapplications of style. Sometimes a bold choice of colour can trick others into believing that my palette is absolutely last minute. And it usually is as I hurtle out the door to work.

And who am I to question the fashion commandments uttered with messianic zeal from the design ziggurats of Milan and Paris? The fashion fascists will insist my taste is more Dimmeys than Dior, more Fosseys than Ferragamo, but I can still dream my Alannah Hill dreams of taffeta and lace, floaty magical confections of diaphanous desire. In the waiting room I can riffle through *Vogue* and *Harper's Bazaar*, looking at the latest offerings and wondering about see-through knees on designer muddied jeans and voluminous swathes of fabric that look fantastic but won't be much chop when doing anything more than posing regally for a fashion shoot. Sometimes, though, it seems I have donned Harry Potter's invisibility cloak; the decree from the fashionistas is that mumsy middle age is not a good look. But I'm not yet ready to march into Millers for the floral top, pastel pants and synthetic cardy that consigns one to the fashion dead-end of nana-land. I still want to be noticed – even if it is only by the nice lady on the tram who compliments me on my flowery hair accessories or the fire engine red jumper or interesting tasselled shawl. And I'm not a

Fella Hamilton woman – just a tad too cosily assured and well-to-do, although I do like the colours. Even labels suggest a demographic uniform and I like to keep people guessing.

Maybe my shape and size just don't shout fashion *élan*. My generous contours are merely hinted at in the gentle flowing folds that suggest mystique and *je ne sais quoi* and the fashion sense acquired over half a century. There is no canyonesque cleavage, no fake tan, not even the hint of cosmetic alteration and adjustment. Just me and the clothes I wear and my fading freckles. All vintage, occasionally chic. My silhouette shrieks solid, not sylph. I am hippy, not hipster.

Perhaps my wisest fashion decision is to stick with what works for me. I can wear classic black or navy and accessorise wildly or with minimalist aplomb. My wardrobe is neither daggy nor cutting edge, but somewhere roomy in the middle – a little bit Country (Road), a touch Target, with a bohemian splash of sartorial insouciance from the Camberwell Market and the great pick up at Vinnies in Mont Albert village. My personal style is mix-and-match, op shop, colour-me-bright, off the peg, kaleidoscopic – my own ever ready-to-wear collection.

A long time ago it was Sportsgirl. It was *never* Portmans. In my twenties I did a great Liz Taylor décolletage and deshabille was *de riguer*. These days I press my nose against the windows of Perri Cutten and wish. Occasionally I wander down Bridge Road,

Richmond to the outlet stores or float through Myer in town and reminisce about the joys of rummaging in the old bargain basement in the late 1970s when I was on a university budget. Laura Ashley served me well in a burnished gold silk wedding dress. It hangs on my clothes rack, between an anorak and a swirly skirt – a reminder that I, too, had my beautiful moment.

It will never be relegated to the dress-up basket.

At the altar of fashion, we catch a whisper of our other selves and settle for who we are. We take what we like and leave the rest to others. We know what works and what doesn't. We make good fashion decisions – most of the time. And we definitely do not want to be invisible. I'm not necessarily aiming for Iris Apfel but I do not want to fade to beige. Now that my ambitions have settled into ones that do not necessarily equate with a certain professional visibility, I have a bright pink streak in my hair. I will not become a rainbow lorikeet or a mad woman, but I will delight in little fashion frills and furbelows, odd brooches or the sweep of unusual colour combinations which fiercely resist the herd mentality of those who must be on trend. Trend is just one step away from tacky.

Bright young things, slender as celery sticks, sashay and stomp as they flick and twirl and then pose robotically. Women of a certain age, with a certain comforting buttery-ness, glide with graceful gait. We've been there – and survived. What was once rock 'n' roll is now rococo. The women in the audience in

Melbourne are just the same as those in Milan and Paris and New York and London. We all want to look good. At the right price for our pockets. But I still stick by that abiding fashion advice from Dale Carnegie: 'The expression on a woman's face is far more important than the clothes she wears on her back.' A smile is always in style.

I've worn frou-frou skirts and boucle jumpers and eye-gouging shoulder pads. I've worn polka dot pinafores, glad rags, lethal stilettos and harem pants. I've worn minis, midis and maxis. I've worn aubergine and teal and mushroom. I've worn my heart on my sleeve. I've zipped myself in so tightly to jeans that I could hardly breathe, but have yet to embrace the girdle as a foundation garment. I have never worn my bra as an outer garment, nor have I worn a bikini. I have never been seen in a tracksuit or Ugg boots. I do have a favourite houndstooth coat that is twenty-two years old and still does the trick. I've not been waxed or polished or abraded. I had my first pedicure in my late forties because it's important for feet to be happy. Unlike my daughter, I have yet to buy anything online because I still like to try things on. These days, though, looking in the mirror takes a bit more courage than it used to, and I prefer low lighting rather than the flagrant fluorescent exposé of all my bumps and dimples. I prefer shopping by myself and have never been one for the posse of girl gang members approving or advising on my fashion choices. There is still that obstinate independent streak, fashion or otherwise; a little bit of pleasing myself and not too worried if others think that my style is a bit hotch-potchy.

As a teenager I was briefly a fashion victim; a slave to others' style statements, but over the years I've created my own. It stands in defiant opposition to all the utterances and ululations from the design gods in their sunbathed studios and gilded emporia. It is what suits me ... and that is not more Melbourne black. With a cup of tea, two dark Chocolate Royals and five minutes to myself I'll see what the department store catalogues are trying to sell me this season.

And then I'll do precisely my own fashion thing!

This is an edited version of an article previously published in *The Secret Garden of Spirituality*.

Everybody has their taste in noises as well as other matters; and sounds are quite innoxious, or most distressing, by their sort rather than their quantity.

JANE AUSTEN, *Persuasion*

Back in 1971 a mellifluously trans-Atlantic spoken-word version of Max Ehrmann's *Desiderata* was a big hit. Part pop-psychology, part poetry-reading, its evocative first lines have always stayed with me: 'Go placidly amid the noise and haste, and remember what peace there may be in silence' (*Desiderata*, 1952).

Today, a lifetime away from the fourteen-year-old I was then, I am going as placidly as possible amidst the noise and haste that seems to furnish much of what passes for life in the twenty-first century. But I can still reach those necessary deep wells of silence that fortify me just when I want to shout, 'Stop the World I Want to Get Off'. I can find peace and quiet when I retreat from the clamour, when I deliberately decide that I am not available, when I choose the occasional visit to family in the country to remind myself that certain noises can be life-giving, not ear-shattering. So the lush loquacity of birds at dawn, the distant hoot of the train leaving Castlemaine, trees swishing in the breeze, the cicada chorus hidden in deep grass, the ruminative moo of milking cows.

Too often we associate noise with ugliness, necessary progress and sometimes danger – the screech of a tyre, the wail of a siren, a threatening shout, a jackhammer breaking concrete or an alarm suddenly going off. It is a jangly jarring discordance that can unsettle and frighten and make the world seem harsher and harder than it really is. The very word 'noise' has a negative connotation when placed next to its much softer-seeming sibling, 'sound', but noise is the product of activity and agency. It is the outcome of doing. We cannot live without it. It is the sound of construction and commerce and traffic, the indelible hum of living in an urban environment where noise means business getting done and people getting from A to B and industry booming. It is the beep of the supermarket register, and the whirr of the coffee machine and the automated school bell at 3.30. It is talkback radio, question time in Parliament (a lot of noise!) and the beep and toot and honk of cars inching along Punt Road, the clapped-out Corolla, the feline Ferrari and the ubiquitous ute. It is the squeal, equal parts thrill and terror, of the Big Dipper, the photocopier clacking in the office and the plane taking off with a rumble that tears the air.

Noise is a doing word.

Neil Diamond knew a thing or two about noise. Beautiful noise. He loved the sound of the street, its buzz and hum, its energy, the locomotion of living. It is life lived out loud. In Melbourne there are certain noises that define the city: the roar of the crowd at the MCG as the ball is bounced on Grand Final Day, the clickety-clack of the W-class tram as it trundles around the CBD, the giant gold timepiece in Melbourne Central as it chimes the hour and plays 'Waltzing Matilda' to locals and tourists, the applause of a theatre crowd and the cry of 'more' echoing from the gods to the stalls. We also experience an almost wordless noise on Anzac morning at the Shrine of Remembrance as thousands walk quietly to the eternal flame, the usual exuberance of a crowd muted by reminiscence and respect. The last watch of the night's deep purple sky holds steady until the first tatters of dawn wake a new day in the metropolis.

And there is the beautiful noise of living in the suburbs. It is the hum and click and tick and tock of the house settling into slumber, exhaling after the rigours of the day and the crazy concerto of family life: Mum reminding about homework; Dad suggesting much better manners; teenage son listening to rap at a level which shakes the walls of his bedroom; daughter practising third grade piano chasing recalcitrant chords across black-and-white keys; toddler laughing and singing 'Baa Baa Black Sheep'; the gathering of friends and the robust debate of contested views, grace being said around the dinner table – the myriad noises of sibling skirmishes, parental admonition, family laughter at a favourite show, the whispered good night as parents check that all are tucked in safely and prayers said so that guardian angels and bed bugs are on notice. It is the noise of tears and tantrums, sometimes of anger and anguish, but more often the sound of the happy ordinariness of easy affection.

I love the sound of the human voice – in love and laughter, at full throttle and in sensitive murmur, in beautiful cadence or elastic euphony. I love the burnished baritone of Russell Crowe's speaking voice and Elvis at his gospel best in 'If I Can Dream'. I love listening to my daughter's happy hobgoblin chortle and her vibrato as she practises her latest audition piece for musical theatre, 'As Long as He Needs Me' from *Oliver!*. I love the noise we make in the bathroom when we try to harmonise Ol' 55's 'Looking for an Echo' or out-scat each other in various versions of 'Summertime'. I love hearing my old school song sung with gusto, Gershwin's 'Rhapsody in Blue', the anthemic build of 'You're the Voice', and the mellow blessing of the cello in a Bach concerto. I love the priest bidding his congregation to lift up their hearts, sending us on our weekly way, a reminder for our small modest hearts to be sacred, not scared, as we encounter the world in all its dimensions.

When we hear favourite hymns or spine-tingling ballads or songs that remind us of happy times when our worlds were a little less serious (Wham's 'Wake Me Up Before You Go-Go' gets a good run here) we know that what we hear can change our mood in a moment. The beautiful noise of a symphony or the lonesome wail of the blues can take us to places we have yet to imagine. Sounds can be soulful.

Whether it is noise or sound is up to us. How we choose to define the aural wallpaper that is an inescapable part of living in the thrust and thrum of this metropolis is a matter of individual response. We can recalibrate the volume register in our lives if we learn to hear and listen differently. The tuneless tinnitus that wears away at our equilibrium can be conquered. It is simply about changing the dial.

We must listen for the good and learn to hear the things that raise us up. Kind words, beautiful music, poetry, encouragement, the thoughts of those who think ahead so that we on this planet might live well, the right and courtesy of inclusive conversation, prayers uttered together that moor us to our faith.

We cannot unhear many things, but we can choose

to minimise their impact so that their hearing does not scar or soil us. We can discern, select, delete.

More than ever, I am aware of the soundtrack to my life with its beautiful noise, sometimes silence, spaces and pauses, grace notes from those with the gifts of music and song. I have often taken my sense of hearing for granted. Now, I am listening more alertly, attuned to the beautiful noise of life as it surges around me. I am not so far away from that fourteen-year-old child of the universe, now happily listening to the music of the world a turnin'.

This is an edited version of an article previously published in *Melbourne Catholic*, November 2018.

We are shaped and fashioned by what we love.

JOHANN WOLFGANG VON GOETHE

Rarely do we celebrate the ordinary, prosaic, uneventful, but enormously graced power of people living good lives in community. However, it is in the usual, routine, sometimes ho-hum and humdrum days of our lives that unseen foundational pillars are cementing the strength that holds us together in more turbulent times. These are communities built on healthy relationships of trust and tolerance, of generosity and good sense, of seeing *the other* in someone else's world view, lifestyle or dress sense and inviting that other to see you in the same neighbourly and equable way. It's about not always judging on appearances or accents or brand names or income, but looking beyond the external to that human person in all their dignity.

Each person in the relationship, whether spouse or sibling, colleague or child must feel valued. They must feel that they matter, that they have a say, that they can actively create their own role in that relationship. Any healthy relationship must be founded on generosity, finding and encouraging the good in others, preferring the positive over the negative. There must also be a healthy dose of reality and a fine seasoning of laughter, rich drizzlings of compassion and a good supply of empathy and that most vital ingredient, love.

Healthy relationships are incubated in the family. A child sees a father doing the dishes after Mum has prepared the meal. The words 'thank you' are always just around the corner, as are words of praise and encouragement. 'Sorry' is more than just a word to say because you were found out. It means a change of action and perhaps a change of heart. Healthy dissent is not to be feared as a family debates the issues of the day in what the Rev David Ransom calls the spirituality of the kitchen table. Children see their parents doing good things in the community and they learn to do those same good things. There is a robust goodness being grown in the exchange of views, the occasional lettings go of tired positions and the emphatic holding on to things that matter.

I met my husband doing a writing course and, as is

often the way with romance, the beans were spilt slowly and carefully over the months of courtship. I was in my mid-thirties, had done the travelling, chambermaiding and bar work all over England, had picked daffodils in Cornwall, run a disco in Guernsey and sold kitchens in Wimbledon. I had sung in a band, cooked in a pub and cleaned at a school. I had sold ice creams, ferried across the Mersey and visited the town of my birth, Nuneaton, in the Midlands. I was back in Melbourne after eight carefree years to sing at my best friend's wedding, a promise I had made to her when our hearts were still young and unbroken.

As we got to know each other I confessed that I wanted to be the best me I could be. In order to find that part of me I had decided to pursue my passion for the written word. So, I enrolled in a year's course at the CAE. He says he fell in love with the sound of my voice and the fact that I delivered an interesting talk to the class on female crime writers. We married six months after our first date; me in spun gold Laura Ashley with a generous décolletage and he in formal black tie and parade gloss black shoes. He still believes, after twenty-five years, that the best of me is imminent.

My daughter, too, knows about the importance of being true to yourself, about finding the best of yourself so that this best is shared with others. My favourite quote is George Eliot's 'It is never too late to be who you might have been'. And so, I persist with love and encouragement and only the occasional groan when I get too precious or forgetful. I do the things that lift my life beyond its demands and dailiness. I look at beautiful paintings, read unfashionable books, dress with a fine disregard for the bland and beige and don't dally over dusting. I am free to be me – no domestic goddess or gourmet cook, but able to do some of the things I love. I'm typing this at 11 pm on a Sunday night with a bit of jazz on in the background and I couldn't be happier!

I'm waiting for my husband to finish his rite-of-passage novel and he's waiting for the Tigers to win another premiership. Our daughter watches Mum and Dad and her uncles and aunts and teachers and other adults doing their bit in the local choir or at the op shop or volunteering their time for those in need. She will learn, I hope, that the best of someone is not something to be kept secret and shrouded, but to be shared so that we all benefit in this goodness, this vast renewable sustainable resource that only humans can create.

I was secretly overjoyed when my daughter got her first part-time job as a waitress and decided to sponsor a World Vision child. She now supports Florence in Rwanda and has done for the last five years. My daughter knows her life chances are better than most people's and that this small effort, equivalent to a new pair of shoes or a couple of breakfasts out, could be life-changing for her sponsored child. Her small change from all those shifts at weekends and during the long holidays is really doing good. Such lessons are the intangibles we pass on, never quite knowing when they will flower in the benevolence of others.

Working out how to be together in a family means compromises, trade-offs, negotiations, a bit of forgiving and forgetting in the mix, listening – the grist of getting the family to work as a unit. I can do a pretty good sulk about things not going my way, but my husband and daughter know just how to dispel my small grievances and furious foot stamping. We accept each other, with our foibles and fancies, penchants and peccadilloes, because we believe in something bigger than the eruptions of ego and the need always to be right.

And we always see the good before the bad.

Children are sponges. They soak up the world around them. If the relationship template they observe or are exposed to is less than ideal, then it will take much rehabilitation to restore it to health. Nor does this mean that generally healthy relationships are soppy and saccharine. Healthy relationships are robust enough to take the odd knock, to be flexible in the changed circumstances of illness or unemployment or lifestyle cutbacks. More recently, the global pandemic has made us all question the quality and viability of many of our relationships, whether intimate, familial or workplace. We have been forced to think about who matters most to us and why.

There have been many tolls caused by COVID-19 and some of these have been to do with long-term relationships which have fractured under the pressures of lockdown, isolation, job loss or the many months of insecurity and anxiety over hotspots and border closures and quarantining. We have all been tested. Sometimes we have found that inner grit and sometimes we have succumbed to tears and fears. Our usual lives, the old normal that we never questioned so blasé were we in our good fortune, has been subjected to a new and prolonged scrutiny where the tiny fissures of familiarity have, for some, become abysses of alienation. Thankfully, most of us have muddled through because we know that although we are flawed and failing, we are also loved and needed. We have also provided a certain constancy for others in these unpredictable times.

Healthy relationships are not based on status, nor calibrated on an income assessment or affordability indicator. Healthy relationships are based on personal, not pecuniary, profiles. They are built on grace and goodwill and the bond of blood that is a binding ingredient. In times like these of economic uncertainty, casualisation or under-employment, it is important to be understanding if a friend or family member is struggling financially or emotionally. This is where we find ourselves today as a community; we need to be vigilant about those who might fall through the cracks or have trouble adjusting to their unexpected circumstances. We have all had much time to think and reflect over the past year and perhaps there is some dismantling of old patterns of thinking and doing in the light of our current situation. We know, more clearly than ever before, what it is that gives our lives meaning and purpose; where we extract the juice and joy that energises and motivates us.

Keeping up with the Joneses is not a yardstick for happiness – but keeping up with those who matter to us is. And we know that our own stories may be impacted by sudden changes – an unexpected redundancy or downsizing, a change in management or the death of a loved one. We are frequently reminded that the only constant is change so we need to be alert, but not alarmed, by the global impacts around us and be ever ready to offer what we can to those who need some certainty in times of doubt and dilemma.

In order to be, we need to be with. We are at our most human in relationships with others. Their love and laughter, encouragement and occasional counselling, grounds and stabilises us. We also acknowledge that relationships are not static; they change as we do, sometimes moving with us, sometimes finding a necessary end. We can still be glad of those relationships we have had in the past that are no longer active in our lives; the ones we have outgrown. They may have been what we needed at that time. We, too, may have been let go, but are still regarded warmly.

Over the past year working from home, Zooming and conducting lessons around the kitchen table, we may have completed something of an audit on the relationships in our lives. We are now readying for healthy new growth all around us. If we can find and affirm the best of each person we meet, be with them in joy and sorrow, in triumph and trial, we are on the way to living out, in our ragged, messy, unpredictable, holy, hopeful and human way, the sacrament of daily existence; the blessedness of each and every day in whatever shape or form it takes.

... And who is my neighbour?

LUKE 10:29

On the noticeboard in the kitchen I have the following poetic quotation pinned up next to timetables, fixtures, bills, reminders and postcards from the past. It is a fragment from the poet, Adam Lindsay Gordon, whose bronze statue is situated next to Parliament House in Melbourne:

> Life is mostly froth and bubble,
> Two things stand like stone.
> Kindness in another's trouble,
> Courage in your own.

I have always admired its sentiment about those perennial standard bearers of the best of the human condition – kindness and courage. Kindness is a word that rarely makes the headlines, as courage often does, but it is the unsung glue that keeps communities together. It is visible in the small actions of wheeling the elderly neighbour's bin in or the larger acts of philanthropy. It's the noticing and listening and doing something for others; sometimes just small things that somehow grease the wheels of community because we recognise, finally, that we help ourselves when we help others. It's the best in us.

The 2019–2020 bushfires scarred lives and landscapes as we learned again the harsh lesson of the beauty and the terror of our homeland. We have mourned the charred cemetery of houses and businesses and schools and churches. Firefighting husbands will never come home again, country kids will worry about the safety of life in the bush and the blue sky swoon of our summers of the past has been replaced by a new narrative that incorporates the unhinged fury of a burning apocalypse.

Our summers will never be the same again.

Our lives are precious and unpredictable. The best laid plans can be undone in moments when things take a sudden unexpected turn and we are left to navigate a different path almost without warning. It is our capacity to do this that testifies to the courage we do not realise we possess when we show grit in the face of the unfair hand we have been dealt. There are times when we surprise ourselves with an inner strength that we did not know we possess until it is tested. Sometimes courage is not the act of bravery, but the quiet and persistent fortitude which says we'll repeat tomorrow what we did today; that an effort will be made to look ahead, to hold your head up and carry on. More than the heroism of the magnificent saving action, which is triggered by accident and adrenaline, the heroism of endurance is something we often miss in the world that devours the big moment and the newsflash. Often it is the quiet moments of rebuilding, avoiding the bitterness of victimhood that can be a natural response to a personal disaster or the outfalls of community dislocation, that tell the world who we really are.

We only have to look at the example of Captain Sir Tom Moore whose efforts, at ninety-nine years of age, raised millions for Britain's National Health Service response to the pandemic. This was the daily courage of walking up and down his backyard with his walking frame to steady him and the knowledge that he was doing something useful. He had no grand design as he went about his humble effort. He did what he could where he was; that simple equation of effort that really does change the course of events and offer hope when days are dark. His generosity of spirit awakened a huge national response and reminded us that hope resides in all of us. Sometimes it is the unexpected figure that reenergises our hearts and reanimates our courage. Real courage, in the adversities of life, can be exhibited at any age and sometimes when we are least prepared for it.

Courage does not have a use-by date.

There are times when life is full of froth and bubble – when we acknowledge the capricious comedy that underwrites the experience of living. We all need some of that lightness in our lives – those moments of laughter or joy or the splendid intersection of happenings which can create a day that sings. We need the comedy of life as a salve against its tragedy. It is another way of relieving pain and allowing us to briefly forget the demands that sometimes make us feel like human husks. We need the chortle and guffaw and the outrageous grin. We need the joke and the good-natured prank. We need some slapstick, wordplay and the occasional prod or poke at the sanctimonious in the form of parody. We need Dame Edna.

However, this very capriciousness can turn into a harsh and unforgiving reality. This is what the world faces now. Within and beyond the borders of our own internal fear and anxiety, widespread and multiplying, we hear voices of end-of-world despair and resignation and a siege mentality. We are told we are on a war footing. We look for guidance. We are infected by the cacophony of calamity and daily doomscrolling.

We are scared.

Since the pandemic began, we have needed to heed voices of common sense and solidarity and kindness. It has been a time to act for the common good. And how gratifying it was to see that the vast majority of Australians understood the necessities of lockdowns and quarantines, even though our economic health took a battering and many people suffered as a result. This is where we have needed courage and kindness in abundance; in families and workplaces and schools and shops. We have needed to gather in the goodness that we saw in the bushfire response and know that we are bigger and better than behaviours that are selfish and opportunistic. We might have been in lockdown, but that does not mean other people were locked out. We have learned to connect in different ways. This has been a time for resetting and reframing and learning to live differently.

Our lives will never be the same again.

As we live out these days that demand our courage and kindness, we must also be ready to accept some change, to innovate, to find ways that mark us as better, graced, giving – a people who think beyond the tiny circle of *mine* to the multiplicities of *ours*. Sometimes change itself takes courage when we have to move on from one mindset or fixed behaviour to another way of seeing or being in the world. We have to let go of inertia or intransigence and open our minds to new encounters and horizons that offer hope. Sometimes courage emerges in the shape of disruption that seeks to improve the lot of those who do not fare as well as we do. We should aim to be people who shelter others; literally and metaphorically. It will be the quick phone call or text, the catch-up coffee and walk or the small talk of greeting and interest that will bind us together in these hard times.

Stone still stands despite fire and flood and disease. Scarred, blackened, pock-marked and weather-beaten; still standing defiantly like that rock of ages, Uluru, hearthed in the middle of our ancient continent.

So, too, the landscape of our hearts.

Kindness and courage.

Still standing like stone, reminding us of who we are and who we can be when it really matters.

The voice of the sea speaks to the soul.
The touch of the sea is sensuous,
enfolding the body in its soft, close embrace.

KATE CHOPIN

In late December, all over this wide brown land, an exodus to the coast begins. Cheek by jowl we park and pack ourselves into tents, caravan parks, chalets and holiday homes and assume a camaraderie long since lost in the suburbs. And just as we desert Melbourne and descend in droves to populate our peninsulas, kamikaze mozzies begin their summer too, landing stealthily to feast on brazenly bare flesh. It's one summer and all summers. It's a quintessential

Australian story – where we prostrate ourselves on the dirty yellow altar of the beach as long blue days curl into a cherished corner of memory.

My memories slip and slide between fact and fiction as I revisit the family holidays of my childhood, colouring in the black-and-white photos of the past. Years merge seamlessly into those before and after it, although I do remember the summer of my fourteenth year, 1971. Long before the good sense of slip-slop-slap, I sunbaked on the Dromana foreshore till I was red raw and blisters festooned my body like bubble wrap. For three days afterwards I was bandaged like a mummy, a poor escaped creature from the backlot of a 1950s horror movie. I remained steadily supine inside whilst my friends pretended not to look at pale skinny boys, rapidly reddening, as they showed off on the beach and Eagle Rock became the backing track to a generation of lives.

Mostly I recall a steadfast swatch of sky and long untroubled days on wide arcs of sand. The beach was an adventure playground where we could squeal and splash and snorkel and run mildly amok without parental admonition. Seaweed garlands tickled my toes as I ducked and dived, a happy water sprite. Sometimes I could overhear the history of the deep as I held a cowrie shell to my ear and was mesmerised by strange siren songs that hinted of unfathomable mysteries; the ancient *deep down things* of Gerard Manley Hopkins' imagining.

My memory is full of snapshots; images and impressions overlapping in messy montage. Buckets and spades, scratchy striped Dickies towels, sticky seats and sticky fingers, ti tree avenues, shallows and sand dunes, the quickstep on baking bitumen, lilos and orange Sunnyboys and long cool chocolate milkshakes, the minstrel nodding of purple agapanthus at the Sisters of Charity holiday house – with chapel – in Mount Eliza that my father secured for two weeks in January, and the long honeyed days of bare skin and rock pools, of calamine lotion and coconut oil.

On holiday, the rhythm of real life is suspended and a languid somnolence replaces more urban urgencies as the obligations and expectations of work and home disappear. Time unspools gently with its minutes and hours generous in their unstructured stretching. The roles of domestic routine are replaced by a certain fluidity, a happy haziness where Mum administers all things BBQ and Dad plays long games of Monopoly while tuned to the cricket. The looser strands of holiday time reign unchallenged as clocks are not watched, emails not checked and meetings not scheduled. We are no longer prisoners to what Michael Leunig calls 'the heartless, dull bureaucracy of time'. Instead, for a few weeks we count time by the heartbeats of summer's sweet benison as we come, pilgrims of all persuasions, to worship at the water.

Down at Rosebud the children paddle in shallows. They toddle tiny-toed out to sandbanks and squeal as they spot a starfish and carefully avoid gelatinous blobs of jellyfish. A small flotilla of black swans glides royally by as the waves create a symphony of water music. In the distance a couple of speedboats skitter lightly on opalescent foam. Freckled mermaids in floral togs frolic in watery resplendence, sun-kissed and happy. Around them their water babies jump for joy in the great blue bath of Port Phillip Bay. The sun shimmers silver on the crest of waves.

The joyful jousting of family life spills out in the raggle-taggle haphazardry of brunches and tippety-run and icy poles and late-night gazing at stars unseen in the city. I wear shapeless T-shirts and old shorts and no make-up. I let myself go. I have time to gather my splintered thoughts, read, relax and be grateful for living here and now. I am surrounded by loved ones and laughter and ready to solve the problems of the world in bibulous late-night discussions with my sisters. I am blessed with the joy of simply being alive.

The beach – that great gritty winding strip of egalitarianism where all can be purified in the frothy font of foam. We are stripped down to our togs and towels and a less self-conscious version of ourselves. We stand before God, ungilded and ungirded, for some ungirdled, just as we are. We are truly girt by sea! We dip and dive and slough off the old year's worries and woes. We submit to the abrasive tingle of the surf and are reborn for the new year. Our sins are washed away in the tide. With this, we emerge dripping and hopeful into the promise of the possible, a year not yet written on ... or written off.

Hopkins must have imagined the sunlit magic of our Christmas holidays when he wrote of bathing as 'summer's sovereign good' and of youth with 'dare and downdolphinry and bellbright bodies' (*Epithalamion*, 1918). How beautiful the bodies of youth, aflame with life, gilded and glad as they dip their toes into adulthood. How beautiful the tableaux of grandparents keeping an eye on water-winged toddlers as they begin to create beach memories. How beautiful all God's children, in their infinite variety, in their multitudinous shapes and sizes, taking to the water and letting it unify them in a gift of simple pleasure.

John Updike writes of the ecstasy and buoyancy of that first summer dive into the sea. He writes that 'swimming offers a parable. We struggle and thrash and drown; we succumb even in despair, and float, and are saved' (*Lifeguard*, June 1962). And so, we surrender helplessly to this transfigurative rite, this collective seasonal baptism, this blessing of the waters. Mermaid forty-year-olds, daggy dads in boardies, jellybean babies, trysting teenagers – there is room for all on the giant gritty welcome mat by the sea.

I bask in the golden grasp of a new, simmering, swashbuckling summer. A tinny tinkling from an ice cream van heralds goodness abroad under the southern sky. Dragonflies kiss daisies. Cicadas serenade the mystical mauve of dusk with a jazzy evensong. Cosmic confetti embroider the night sky comfortingly and a liquid lullaby laps the shore.

On holiday, I give thanks for long, loose-limbed days and late nights skin-deep with warmth. I will hold them close as the rest of the year begins to demand my attention and time is no longer my own. These snapshot memories will sustain me when my inbox is full, a deadline is looming, corrections hover and there are not enough hours in the day for all I want to do.

Centuries ago, the Bard opined, 'Summer's lease hath all too short a date'. Yes, we live different lives in the heat of these few short weeks as another summer is added to the infinite almanac of heavenly blue days.

And all across the nation sandcastles are imagined, built and washed away, their turrets tumbling to the tide.

This is an edited version of an article previously published in *Melbourne Catholic*, December 2018.

*What wisdom can you find that
is greater than kindness?*

JEAN-JACQUES ROUSSEAU

As the year winds down and the festivities step up, the season of the annual review begins. This is about how the year has been for us professionally, whether or not we have accomplished set goals, what went well and what could be improved. It's a report card of the adult variety. These evaluations often come under the dreaded acronym KPI – Key Performance Indicator.

Sometimes the process can be affirming and sometimes there are elements of anxiety involved if what you believe you have achieved may not be seen to satisfy managerial requirements. Sometimes what matters is not even counted. However, we are not just workers in various institutions subject to different bureaucratic demands that make decisions about our agency in the workforce. Thank God, we are all more than functionaries, cookie-cutter clones or automatons. We are gloriously holy and imperfect human beings jostling and bumping along together on the road of life.

We also happen to be Christian or Muslim or Jewish or people of other faith traditions. Or we may not have a faith background but know that we have a moral code that motivates us towards goodness. For us, there could be another standard worth examining. This is not simply a measure of some feel-good altruism, but a way of confirming that we live with an everyday holiness that demands that we love our neighbour as ourselves.

This is the Kindness Performance Indicator.

One of the workplace kindnesses I often see is when a colleague, instead of just checking and collecting material from their pigeonhole, has a quick squiz to see if their colleagues' pigeonholes also need clearing. Material is quietly delivered to the recipients' desks, saving them a trip down two flights of stairs in the middle of a busy day. Such kindnesses are the lubricants of collegiality, little grace notes that make a workplace warm.

A small kindness might be noticing that someone

needs a moment to themselves or a gentle hug. They might need the acknowledgement that we are with them emotionally, prayerfully, during difficult times. Saying 'We are praying for you' is a special sort of kindness understood by people of faith. Even cheerfulness is a kindness when an atmosphere is gloomy.

Saint Thérèse of Lisieux championed 'The Little Way', a model of practising everyday acts of saintliness for those of us who are not in the position to make grand or heroic gestures. She wrote: 'Miss no single opportunity of making some small sacrifice, here by a smiling look, there by a kindly word, always doing the smallest right and doing it all for love.'

A small kindness might be a quick note or a bunch of flowers or muffins made for a morning tea. It might be sitting next to the new person at a meeting or making a coffee for someone who is harried. It could be doing something for which there will be no appreciation and perhaps even mockery or derision or a metaphorical slap in the face. This is when kindness really counts. The God who notices the lilies and the sparrows sees especially those acts which are done without the witness of an audience; the acts that tell of who we are in the privacy of our true hearts.

Colossians 3:12 reminds us, 'Therefore, as God's chosen people, holy and dearly loved, clothe yourselves with compassion, kindness, humility, gentleness and patience.' As we embrace each new year with its plans, schemes and to-do lists etched into its unfolding days and weeks, perhaps these rebadged KPIs can measure who we truly say we are.

This is an edited version of an article previously published in *Australian Catholics*, Summer 2018/2019.

Acknowledgements

A book never arrives without many hands and hearts helping it into the world. These are those who believe in its purpose and what it can offer the reader by way of its content and ideas. *Blessed* has been blessed by the editorial nurturing of Elizabeth Harrington whose fine eye and thoughtful suggestions enhanced the flow and impulse of the book. Publisher Regina Lane was actively involved in shepherding this project to fruition and she and Liz were in frequent contact with me to check minor details and wording and to ensure that the feel of the book was exactly what I wanted.

I would also like to acknowledge those editors in the past who have dealt with my submissions, sometimes planned, often on spec, with sensitivity and common sense. Thanks to Michael McVeigh from *Australian Catholics*, David Halliday while at *Melbourne Catholic* and Susan Kurosawa, when she was Travel and Indulgence editor at *The Australian*. They took my work and shaped it for wider publication.

I have been encouraged by those family, friends, colleagues, parents, students, neighbours and strangers who have said something affirming, contacted me, remarked on a particular phrase, cut out a column to put on the fridge (next to a Leunig cartoon, I hope, so I am glad of that company) or asked me to write something special for their group, school or community.

Writers need to know that their words find a receptive audience.

My parents and teachers were always encouraging of me and I hope that I lift the aspirations and talents of those I teach. My four sisters and two brothers are supportive of my wordy ways and readily keep me in order if I get a little uppity. I would especially like to thank my sister, Fiona O'Neill, for her beautiful artwork adorning the cover of *Blessed*. Finally, my husband, Robert, knows that I am happiest when I am scribbling at a café, under the Dome at the State Library or at the kitchen table in the late hours. My daughter, Grace, knows that I love words and she wouldn't have me any other way. They barrack for me enthusiastically and understand my flights of fancy.

I am indebted to all those writers whose work nourishes my own creative impulse and I am glad that I can make my own small contribution. I hope that something here strikes a chord, raises a smile or sparks another story. This is what it's all about – writing my way into the world and sharing it happily with others.

I couldn't ask for more.

www.ingramcontent.com/pod-product-compliance
Lightning Source LLC
Chambersburg PA
CBHW032335300426
44109CB00041B/807